DON COLSON

QUIET
COURAGE

Stories of the Unselfish Dedication of Maine Veterans

Quiet Courage: Printed by J.S. McCarthy Printers

INTRODUCTION: FROM THE SPONSOR OF THE BOOK

One of the most important missions of the Cole Land Transportation Museum has long been to recognize and honor the nation's military veterans, who, by sharing their wartime experiences with students, help inspire young people in Maine and elsewhere to summon within themselves the strength, character, and integrity essential to a truly meaningful and productive life.

Thousands of students and their teachers statewide have participated in our unique veteran interview program since it began in 1992. Yet, as the aging population of World War II, Korean, and Vietnam Veterans dwindles, our mission to keep their heroic stories alive grows more challenging with each passing year.

Having witnessed scores of these interviews and the spirited discussions they've generated among young and old, I felt that the veterans' real-life accounts should be preserved for posterity in a book.

Longtime friend, military veteran and former TV anchor Don Colson agreed to write it, and it turned out to be a match that has exceeded my expectations.

In gratitude for their military service and service here, veteran patriots were invited to become part of this project. Many accepted, and their stories including those of other veterans from throughout Maine, create a compelling historical legacy that we hope will enlighten and inform generations of young people in Maine and the rest of the country.

So thank you, Don, not only for taking on this worthy challenge, but for your hard work and dedication that has made it so successful.

We extend heartfelt thanks to veterans everywhere, including my deceased squad members, other personal friends, and all who have proudly served our country, in all its conflicts.

On behalf of the more than 100 volunteers at the GALEN COLE FAMILY FOUNDATION, AND COLE LAND TRANSPORTATION MUSEUM, we dedicate this book to ALL VETERANS.

Galen L. Cole, Founder

To all who served.

FOREWORD
United States Senator Susan M. Collins

In his First Inaugural Address, Abraham Lincoln spoke of the "mystic chords of memory, stretching from every battlefield and patriot grave to every living heart and hearthstone all over this broad land..." As America faced its gravest crisis, those magnificent words were a reminder that the freedom that blessed our nation had been won and defended by ordinary citizens possessing the extraordinary traits of courage, devotion to duty, and sacrifice.

Those mystic chords resonate through the pages of this book. From the battlefields of Europe and the Pacific more than six decades ago, to Korea, Vietnam, Somalia, Afghanistan, and Iraq, the brave men and women of Maine have earned a place of honor in the hearts of all who cherish freedom. Some of the stories here are amusing; some are heartbreaking; all are inspiring. I salute Don Colson for telling them so expertly and lovingly.

This great project is made possible by the tireless efforts of one of Maine's greatest veterans and citizens. The promise Galen Cole made on a battlefield in Germany to dedicate his life to his community and fellow man is one he has fully kept. His generosity in providing a copy of this book to every school and public library in our state is but one example of the astonishing energy and enthusiasm Galen puts into everything he undertakes.

The title of this book is significant. One of the distinguishing traits of America's veterans is their modesty - the quiet courage evident in every chapter. That trait has never been described more succinctly than it is here by Everett Pope, a Medal of Honor winner during World War II: "When the war ended, I put the sword down and came home."

All the stories in this book are inspiring, but one is to me deeply personal; the story of my father, Don Collins. Growing up, I knew he had served in World War II, but the details-of combat, of valor, of friendships made, and of friends lost, he kept to himself. When the war ended, he "put the sword down and came home."

One of my earliest childhood memories is of my Dad taking me to the Memorial Day parade in my hometown of Caribou. He would wear his tattered old Army jacket and hoist me high on his strong shoulders. From that wonderful vantage point, I could see hats come off and hands go over hearts up and down the street as the flag passed by.

The stories in this book are strong shoulders from which we, and generations to come, can see the courage, devotion to duty, and sacrifice of the men and women who have worn the uniform of the United States of America. From this wonderful vantage point, we can hear those mystic chords that are our past, our present and--as long as we continue to listen-our future.

FOREWORD
Governor John Baldacci

From the very earliest days of this country, Maine's men and women have answered the call to serve. During our darkest days – whether in the shadow of Pearl Harbor or standing atop the rubble of 9/11 – Mainers have stood resolute in the face of terrible peril, risking, and too often giving their lives for the sake of others.

Don has undertaken an enormous task in trying to document the lives and memories of these brave men and women.

Through exhaustive research and personal interviews, we get a chance to meet some of our state's veterans, to hear their stories in their own words and to get to know them as individuals. We learn about their hopes, their dreams and the difficulties they faced.

Their stories are deeply personal and often inspirational, and should be a reminder to all of us as we toil about our daily lives, that others before us have given much to lift us up.

History is catching up with many of our veterans, especially those who served during World War II. Our grandchildren, removed by generations from that great struggle, won't remember, firsthand, the sacrifice necessary to save the world from the tyranny of Nazism or the horrors faced on chunks of rocks like Iwo Jima in the South Pacific.

They aren't likely to meet many women like Sgt. Delores Hainer, who joined the Women's Army Corps in 1949 and who lost a brother-in-law in the Korean War. And hopefully they'll never know the terror faced by Delmont Merrill as he stormed ashore on Iwo Jima with a flame thrower strapped to his back.

It's important that the bravery and sacrifices, of all Mainers, in all conflicts, from WW II, to Korea, Vietnam, the deserts of the Middle East, and other trouble spots, not be forgotten.

The passage of time does not absolve us of our responsibility to remember. Don's book carries forward these stories of ordinary men and women, called to do extraordinary things.

Maine has about 150,000 veterans, 105,000 who served in combat. Those Soldiers, Sailors, Airmen and Marines have been asked to do much during this country's wars. Don has helped protect their legacy and preserve it for posterity.

CONTENTS

CONTENTS

CONTENTS

CONTENTS

CONTENTS

50TH ANNIVERSARY OF THE END OF WW II
SEPTEMBER 2, 1995

Veterans Remembrance Bridge, September 2, 1995
Vietnam Veterans of America, First Maine Chapter #185

The U.S. Veterans Friends, Group, (Below) from Luxembourg.

The Madawaska High School Band, (Above) left home at 3:20 A.M. to be in the parade.

Photos this page: Courtesy Cole Museum

PREFACE

A few years ago, my wife Brenda and I drove through the battleground at Gettysburg. I've wanted to do that for a long time. The terrain is a lot different today. There were far fewer trees in 1863; less cover.

We drove slowly, along that long road through the battlefield, by all the monuments, New York, Virginia, Massachusetts, and all the others. I tried to imagine what it was like there in 1863; 172,000 Americans fighting each other, 75,000 on the Confederate side....97,000 fighting for the Union; farmers, carpenters, ship workers, woodsmen..... A slight breeze replaced the blast of cannons. No way to really imagine. 51,000 Americans died in the Battle of Gettysburg.

When we came to "Little Round Top" we stopped and got out. It's just a short walk through the woods to the knoll where General Joshua Chamberlain and the 20th Maine took their stand. It was the second day of the battle, July 2nd, 1863; the battle that changed the course of the Civil War. There's a simple marker on the spot today.

I thought about Joshua Chamberlain. What was he really like? The farmers, carpenters, ship workers, and woodsmen who were with him. What would the soldiers of the 20th Maine tell us about themselves, if we could speak with them? Of course we can't anymore.

I had two uncles who fought in World War One. Ralph Clement and Austin Heath fought in the trenches. They both went over the top at "Meuse-Argonne." Both were decorated for their actions during WW I. I didn't speak with them for a second about their experiences. What a loss!

That's why I like the "Veteran Interview Program" at the Cole Land Transportation Museum so much. Each year dozens of veterans volunteer their time to be interviewed by Maine school children. The students learn about important chapters in our history from the people who were there. They learn about the terrible price paid by everyone. They learn how precious "Freedom" really is, from the people who put their lives on the line to protect our freedom. Their experiences and their thoughts are not being lost.

That's why I got such satisfaction out of writing this book. Oh, it's not my idea. Galen Cole asked me to write it, to pay tribute to these great Americans....to acknowledge their heroism.....their sacrifices. He arranged to have it published. He made it happen, as he does with lots of good things. Thanks Galen for asking me to do it. It was a much more rewarding project than I could possibly imagine.

A quick "cop-out" to the vets and everyone who reads this book. I'm not an author, and I don't pretend to be. I spent thirty-five years writing for television.... conversationally; the way we speak. Everything was written in capitol letters. It's easier to read on television that way. We didn't worry much about quotes or any other punctuation. I was taught to write as I talk. As years passed it became easier to talk and tell stories, rather than read. I never got to the point where I could totally remove myself from the stories anyway. I care about people. I make no apologies for that.

I've tried hard to eliminate errors in grammar, and spelling and such things, but you'll probably find a few. Please don't let that get in the way of learning about the great Mainers, this book is about.

You also need to know, there is no planned order for the people you will meet in this book. I interviewed them as I learned about them. Yes, I did intentionally look for more veterans of WW II than the others, because we're losing them. I wanted to learn about them and introduce them to you before they're all gone.

There's no great plan to the sequential order in the way they are arranged in the book. I tried to group them by the combat period they were in. That's a bit complicated too. As you'll read, many served in WW II and Korea. Many others served in Korea and Vietnam; you get the idea. Please just know, together, they are all patriotic Mainers and when their country needed them, every single one of them stepped forward and served.

Just a couple more notes:

As the project went on, I learned about more veterans who certainly deserve to be in this book but aren't. I apologize, to them, for not including them. I flat ran out of space. I hope someday someone will write another book. There are lots more great stories to be told.

And a note about the heroes who are in the book and probably my greatest frustration: How do you possibly tell the story of anyone who did what these veterans did, in a few short pages? Many spent two and three decades serving their country, honorably. The answer is, you don't. I have simply picked chapters of their lives that, at least, introduce these extraordinary people to you. I hope I have chosen well.

Don Colson

QUIET COURAGE
Stories of the Unselfish Dedication of Maine Veterans

"Operation Desert Storm" began the morning of January 17, 1991. Our attack was conducted from the air for the first weeks. Missiles...planes.

On February 9, 1991, elements of the 2nd Brigade, 1sts Cavalry Division entered Iraq...within days thousands of coalition forces would follow. On February 22, 1991, Iraq agreed to a Soviet proposed cease-fire.

American casualties during the Gulf War (1990-1991)

Battle deaths...............................147
Other deaths 1,947*
Americans wounded......................467

Operation Gothic Serpent was fought on October 3 and 4, 1993, in Mogadishu, Somalia. The United States was trying to get food and medical supplies to over three million Somali people who were displaced by warring clans. The Somalis were starving to death. Our humanitarian efforts were crushed by war-lords, who were followers of Mohamed Farrah Aidid.

On October 3rd, a US task force of several special forces units, attempted to enter Mogadishu and capture leaders of Aidid's militia. During the operation, two US Black Hawk helicopters were shot down by rocket-propelled grenades, and three others were damaged. Some of the soldiers were able to evacuate the wounded, but others were trapped at the crash sites.

Lincoln, Maine native, US Army, Master Sergeant, Gary Gordon was killed in the battle that followed. Gordon received a "Medal of Honor" for his courageous action.

American casualties during the Battle of Mogadishu
Battle deaths....................................18
(Another American soldier was killed in a mortar attack two days later.)
Americans wounded...........................73

*"Other deaths" Service members who died, but not as a result of combat.

"Operation Enduring Freedom" was the US government's military response to the September 11, 2001 attacks on the United States. On October 7th, a little more than a month, after the attack at the World Trade Towers and the Pentagon, the US began combat action in Afghanistan. The prime targets were terrorist training camps, and the capture of al-Qaeda leaders. Our mission was to stop terrorist activities in that country. The terrorists, who hi-jacked the planes on September 11[th,] trained at camps in Afsghanistan.

American casualties during Operation Enduring Freedom
Battle deaths..............................353
Americans wounded...................1,102

"Operation Iraqi Freedom" officially began on March 20, 2003. US officials thought Iraqi President Saddam Hussein was manufacturing chemical and biological weapons, and possibly even nuclear weapons. That proved to be untrue. Hussein's infamous sadistic treatment of his people was widely known.

A coalition, of mostly US forces, invaded Iraq. Baghdad fell on April 9, 2003. Hussein escaped but was subsequently captured by US troops on December 13, 2003. He was tried and convicted of "Crimes against Humanity." Hussein was hanged by the new Iraqi government on December 20, 2006. As this book went to printing in 2007, the casualty count from "Iraqi Freedom" was still rising.

American casualties during "Iraqi Freedom"
(As of March 20, 2007)
Battle deaths....................3,218
Battle deaths – Maine.............16
Americans wounded.........32,544

Notes: Casualty figures vary for all our wars. The statistics listed in this book are the most commonly reported, according to the Department of Defense and Veterans Administration.

Many of the people in this book, served in several combat periods. I have grouped them in one of their prominent eras.

OPERATION IRAQI FREEDOM

Kuwait March, 2004
Members of the 152nd Field Artillary, Maine Army National Guard, prepare to ship out to Baghdad.
Back row (L-R) Allen-Glenburn, Jackson-New Orleans, Grivois-Oakland, Thorndike-Vinal Haven, Horton-Waterville
Front (L-R) Pease-Waterville, Knight-Orono, Rediker-Levant
Photo: Courtesy Mark Rediker

DUSTIN JAMES HARRIS

Patten, Maine

U.S. Army........................June 2004 – April 6, 2006

SPC., Airborne Infantry (Stryker Brigade)

Lorna Harris – Dustin's Mom:
"He loved what he was doing."

Spc. DUSTIN JAMES HARRIS
May 11, 1984 - April 6, 2006

7

November 2005, he got the call again, and this time there was no doubt, he was heading for "Iraqi Freedom:"...Baghdad, Fallujah, the Sunni triangle.....insurgents, terrorists, roadside bombs!

He could have turned it down. His wife Jenn was pregnant with their second child. Brian had already had one foreign assignment; but he didn't turn it down. He couldn't turn his back on his guys, he says; couldn't turn his back on, "Everything I've done my entire five years in the Marine Corps. Here I am in charge of these guys.... training them. I couldn't do it to the guys. I couldn't do it to myself."

Blue Hill, September 2006
Marine Cpl. Brian Smith and his wife Jenn with their two children, 8-year old Raine and 8-month old Haven at their Blue Hill home in September, 2006.
Photo: Courtesy "The Ellsworth American" Photographer: James Straub

That's why his team was on that road outside Fallujah, Iraq, on August 24th, 2005. He told me what happened.

"We were on patrol. On that particular day, I ended up taking the most dangerous seat in the convoy, which is the first vehicle.... commander's seat."

Brian Smith in Iraq 2006
Photos: Courtesy Brian Smith

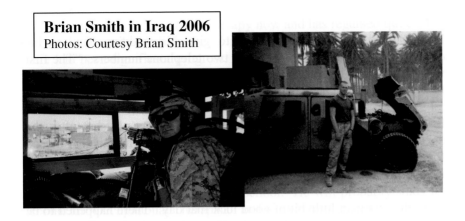

There was a convoy up in front of us, heading south, while we were heading northbound. My driver started to pull over, a little bit more to the right side of the road, and we hit an "I.E.D." (*Improvised explosive device.*)

It blew the Humvee to the middle of the road.

"I don't think I got knocked out......just for a second there, I......holy hell what happened!"

He looked around, to check on his men. They were fine; and that's when he saw his arm.

"It didn't look right, and I said oh, this ain't good. I tried to move it and it didn't move. I reached down to see if it was still there...I felt blood squirting my hand, eighteen inches away."

A large piece of shrapnel had torn right through the upper muscles of his right arm, cutting an artery. Brian, who was pinned in the vehicle, could bleed to death in minutes.

While he squeezed his right arm with his left hand, a pressure point he learned in his Marine training, he propped a radio and computer system against his back, for leverage and, "I just kept kicking the door and it finally opened."

He lost so much blood, he was barely conscious, when they got him to the hospital.

"I thought I was going to lose my arm."

THE DESERT WARS AND TERRORISM

September 11, 2001 – A KC-135E, from the 101st Air Refueling Wing of the Maine Air National Guard, is first over New York City, after the terriorist attack on the World Trade Towers. The fighters are from the 102nd Fighter Wing, Otis Air National Guard Base, Massachusetts
Photo: Courtesy 102nd Fighter Wing

DEBORAH ALLEY

Stonington, Maine

U.S. Air Force...............November 6, 1978 – December 13, 1992
Maine Air National Guard.....December 1998 – February 2005

Master Sergeant, Information Management

Her sons, 1st Lieutenant Robert Anthony Effler II, and August Ramon Oniell............Both Active Duty, U.S. Air Force

"The Air Force was outstanding!"

All the stories in this book are about veterans........military people; The story of Debbie Alley is about a woman who is about as military as military can be; from her dad Ranson Runkles who served with the Marines in China and Burma, during WW II, and her uncle Truman Runkles who was in the "Battle of the Bulge," to her husband Ron who was in the Air Force when she met him while she was on active duty, and her two sons who are in the Air Force today.

August's graduation from Pararesque Indoc Tng. October 13, 2006.

Lackland Air Force Base
M/Sgt Debbie Alley and her sons, A1C August Oniell (L)
and 1st Lt Robert Effler II (R)
Photo: Courtesy Debbie Alley

17

Two years later 2/4 went ashore in the Dominican Republic when the government there was unable to end the treat against US Citizens. The Marines ended it.

Since that day, World War One, World War Two, Vietnam and all the other trouble spots, Second Battalion, Fourth Marines have been on the front lines. The battalion was reactivated for Korea, but hostilities ended before they got there.

Today, they're back at the front again, in all the "Desert Wars."

January 1991, Bill Jones was in the desert in Saudi Arabia, ready to go against Saddam Hussein's Republican Guard in Kuwait.

"We had just got done playing a game of "Spades." The TV came on… CNN showed American Troops deployed to Saudi Arabia." Bill was on his second Mediterranean cruise.

That's how his battalion operated. Six months on a ship in the Mediterranean, "You're basically the "911" force," ready to respond. Then they'd come home, for six months, to train and prepare for the next cruise. He was on his second "Med" cruise when Iraqi forces moved into Kuwait.

August 2nd, 1990, five days after Iraqi forces moved into Kuwait, the United States started to deploy forces to Saudi Arabia. (Operation Desert Shield) The organization of a coalition of forces from other countries had already begun. There was world wide agreement, that Iraqi troops must be driven out of Kuwait. There was fear, the Iraqis had other plans too…like Saudi Arabia.

Bill Jones unit returned to Camp Lejeune, North Carolina in December from his "Med" cruise. "We were put on air alert." They were restricted to base, ready to be deployed immediately.

His parents and sister came to Camp Lejeune for Christmas. "Probably the most memorable Christmas I ever experienced." A last chance to see him before he was deployed to the "Sand Box." He was heading for combat. The unspoken fear… possibly a last chance to see him?

December 31st the order came. Bill remembered the words of his drill instructor from basic training. 'Some of you will make it in my Marines; some of you will not make it in my Marines. Some of you will be killed in combat.' Bill celebrated New Year's Eve on the plane, on the way over. "We landed at Camp 15, Al Jabayl, Saudi Arabia on January 1ˢᵗ."

If there was any doubt about what they were getting into, it was quickly removed. "We always had to have our flack jackets and helmets on." They learned to take care of their weapons in the sand. Bill had a 50 caliber machine gun and a 40 mm machine gun on a Humvee. "We used to dig holes in the sand…take our ponchos with bungee cords and put it over the hole." Keep a low profile in the sand. Their vehicles were staggered and dug in.

Saudi Arabia-January 1991
William Jones Jr, by his desert sleeping quarters.
The cards he's holding are the first mail he received from his parents and sister.
Photo: Courtesy Bill Jones

They expected to be there for several weeks while supplies arrived. "We were rolling with our gear in a week and a half…heading north." Mission...liberate Kuwait City.

January 17, 1991, "Operation Desert Storm" began. "I can remember sitting in my turret at night, watching the sorties and at two o'clock in the morning, watching B-52 runs." Early February, ground forces began to move. "My machine gun team was providing security for the Am-Tracks as they went through the breeches." They engaged the Republic Guard just south of the Kuwaiti border. "We were taking prisoners. There were fire fights, yeah." The region was blanketed by thick oil smoke, and artillery explosions rumbled across the area.

Saudi Arabia
Bill Jones during Desert Storm, 1991.
Photo: Courtesy Bill Jones

On February 22ⁿᵈ, the Iraqis agreed to a Soviet proposed cease fire.

Like too many others, Bill came home to deal with the horrible memories of war. Thanks to the people at the Veteran's Center in Bangor, he's doing it. "Those guys down there are life savers." Bill's fully disabled because of the "PTSD" (*Post Tramatic Stress Disorder*) but that doesn't mean unproductive.

In addition to significant time spent on behalf of the Marine Corps League, he helps out with Toys for Tots, and several other charities. A fair amount of time is volunteered too, as part of the Marine Color Guard, in parades, at funerals and other functions.

He's also an avid outdoorsman…hunts and fishes.

And in spite of the PTSD, he might be the biggest advocate for the US Marines anywhere. "I'm proud to say that I did serve over there." Would you do it again? "In a heartbeat!"

Korean War Memorial, Memorial Day 2006.
Marine Corp League Color Guard. Bill Jones
is 2nd from the left.
Photo: Courtesy Bill Jones

GARY GORDON

Lincoln, Maine

U.S. Army..................Killed in Action – October 3, 1993

Master Sergeant, Special Forces. (Medal of Honor recipient.)

"a tiny fraternity whose common bond is uncommon valor."
John Marsh, Secretary of the Army (His quote is inscribed on a stone in front of the Lincoln Town Office.)

Gary Gordon was part of the tiny fraternity of Special Forces in the military; "Delta Force." On October 3rd, 1993 he was part of a force sent into Mogadishu, Somalia, to capture leaders of war-lord Mohamed Farrah Aidid's militia.

Master Sergeant Gary Gordon
U.S. Army Special Forces
August 30, 1960 – October 3, 1993

For two years, after the overthrow of Dictator Mohammed Siad Barre, several warring tribes were trying to grab power in Somalia. Agriculture had been destroyed. More than twenty thousand had been killed in the fighting. Many, many more people died from starvation...some estimates exceed 500,000 people died. "Operation Provide Relief" began in August 1992, when the Bush White House joined UN efforts to provide relief. It didn't work. Food continued to be stolen, and brought to clan leaders, who exchanged it with other countries for weapons.

Further attempts by United Nations forces to implement disarmament led to more violence. June 5, 1993, twenty-four Pakistani troops were killed in an area of Moagadishu controlled by Aidid. The next day the United Nations Security Council issued Resolution 837, calling for the arrest and trial of the people responsible for the ambush. October 3rd, 1993 the plan was together....forces were in place...

"Task Force Ranger" headed out....US Special Operations Forces composed of Ranger teams, Army Delta Force and Navy SEALs with support from the 160th Aviation Regiment headed for Mogadishu to capture Aidid's top advisors.

Black Hawk "Super 64"

Mike Durant's helicopter over the Somali coast on October 3, 1993.
Photo: US Special Forces Command

The mission ran into trouble almost immediately. Ground convoys, which were to take the captured ministers out, were blocked by Somali citizens. A five ton truck, part of the convoy, was hit by a rocket-propelled grenade. Two Black Hawk helicopters were shot down.

When Gary Gordon learned ground forces were not available to protect the second chopper and the four injured crew members, he and Sergeant First Class Randall Shughart volunteered to be dropped at the site, already surrounded and under heavy fire by enemy forces. After their third request Gordon and Shughart were given permission to proceed.

The citation awarding the "Medal of Honor toM/Sgt. Gary Gordon reads in part:

"Equipped with only his sniper rifle and a pistol, Master Sergeant Gordon and his fellow sniper, while under intense small arms fire from the enemy, fought their way through a dense maze of shanties and shacks to reach the critically injured crew members. Master Sergeant Gordon immediately pulled the pilot and other crew members from the aircraft, establishing a perimeter which placed him and his fellow sniper in the most vulnerable position. Master Sergeant Gordon used his long range rifle and side arm to kill an undetermined number of attackers until he depleted his ammunition. Master Sergeant Gordon then went back to the wreckage, recovering some of the crew's weapons and ammunition. Despite the fact that he was critically low on ammunition, he provided some of it to the dazed pilot and then radioed for help. After his team member was fatally wounded and his own rifle ammunition exhausted, Master Sergeant Gordon returned to the wreckage, recovering a rifle with the last five rounds of ammunition and gave it to the pilot with the words, "good luck." Then, armed with only his pistol, Master Sergeant Gordon continued to fight until he was fatally wounded. His actions saved the pilot's life."

The pilot, Mike Durant told a reporter for "American Valor" on PBS, "Without a doubt, I owe my life to these two men and their bravery. These guys came in when they had to know it was a losing battle." He said of Gordon and Shughart, "There was nobody else left to back them up. If they had not come in, I wouldn't have survived." Sergeant First Class Randall Shughart was also awarded the "Medal of Honor" posthumously.

Gary's mother Betty told me, he was good in school. He played football; liked sports. She says she may have gotten her earliest impression of his true personality when she went to a parent teacher's conference when

Gary was in the 5th grade, "The only problem they had with him....he liked to draw, and he was drawing all the time in school. The only thing he would draw was military jeeps, military vehicles, and helicopters." That's where his heart was, even then.

On Sunday, July 23, 1995 the town of Lincoln dedicated a memorial, on the town office lawn, to Gary Gordon. The inscription reads, "**In Memory of Master Sergeant Gary Gordon, U.S.Army Special Forces, Aug. 30, 1960 – Oct 3, 1993, awarded the Medal of Honor for 'extraordinary heroism' with which he fought and died in effort to rescue comrades in Somalia. 'In Delta's ranks is a special breed...they belong to a tiny fraternity whose common bond is uncommon valor."**

John Marsh, Secretary of the Army

Lincoln, Maine

The Memorial Stone on the Town Office lawn at 63 Main St., dedicated to the memory of M/Sgt Gary Gordon.
Photo: Town of Lincoln

PETER AND JOHN D'ERRICO

Bangor, Maine

Peter:
U.S. Air Force.............................March 1956 – March 1959
Maine Air National Guard...........April 1959 – November 1978

Major, Navigator/Weapons Systems Officer

John:
Maine Air National Guard...September, 1978 – On active dty

Colonel, Pilot/Vice Wing Commander

"It took a lot of guts for a city of thirty-thousand people."

Peter D'Errico and John D'Errico......father and son: together they have served their country, their state and their city, more than seventy years.....all because a guy from Brooklyn needed to be in the northeast.

It's Peter, who says his career with the military was "unremarkable." You have to know Peter to know he's low key, and quite inclined to dismiss his accomplishments. No he didn't fire a shot in anger during his service years. Our country didn't get attacked. For most of his career, Peter was a "Back Seater" in fighter jets. He flew in F-89's and F-101st for the 132nd Fighter Interceptor Wing out of Bangor. I think it's more than possible that we didn't get attacked, and Peter didn't fire a shot in anger, because people like Peter were on alert, ready to defend their country.

Bangor, Maine
Weapons Control Officer, Major Peter D'Errico in the cockpit of an f-89J.
Photo: Courtesy Peter D'Errico

He received his Air Force commission when he completed the ROTC program and graduated from New York University in 1953. Peter went to navigator training and because he was at the top of his class, he got his pick of assignments. "My father died while I was in the Air Force. My mother was 42 years old. I had two younger brothers. She was a typical housewife, no driver's license, no previous employment. I had to get to a place that would be as close to them as possible." He considered Pease Air Force Base in New Hampshire, but housing was scarce there, so he chose Dow Field, Bangor, Maine.

Peter D'Errico at his Bangor home. November 2006. The models on the bookcase in the background are planes Peter flew in.
Photo: Don Colson

Peter was navigator on KC-97's while he was on active duty: the old four engine refueling planes. The Maine Air Guard was part of the Air Defense Command, when he left active duty. That meant fighter jets. Peter trained to be a "Weapons Systems Operator" and flew in the back seat, until he retired from the guard in 1978.

He stayed in Bangor. Bangor knew already the guy from Brooklyn was a keeper. Peter will say he was just one of many people, but in fact he played a major role in the metamorphosis of Bangor from a military town to a civilian aviation, economic center.

It was 1964, when the Federal Government announced that Dow Air Force base was on the closure list. Hardly a person, who was around, will forget the day. Thirteen thousand people were directly involved with Dow. That's how many moved away. The base contributed a great deal more to the local economy. It's an understatement to say it was a major blow!

Peter was Industrial Development Director of Bangor at the time. The city was already planning a major "Urban Renewal" project. Peter says, "We had to relocate a lot of companies...like N.H. Bragg, like Snow and Neally, like Bangor Hardware.

He's quick to point out, "It wasn't the city that took that railroad station away. A group of businessmen bought it and tore it down." For about forty years, the city has been criticized for the loss of the majestic old building. Peter agrees, "It could have been restored to something really nice and of historic significance."

Dow Field officially closed in July of 1968. It's not surprising that Economic Development Director and part time Air National Guard member Peter D'Errico would become Airport Director in 1970. "I knew the language of aviation because of my military experience. We were on the great circle route to Europe. Our first objective was to see if we could interest aircraft into looking at us if they had to divert."

He says there were a couple of very important things in their favor. First, "We already had Northeast Airlines, a major commercial carrier, and our Air National Guard Unit operated out of the airport. Because of that, the FAA would continue to man the tower." Probably most important of all, "They (*The guard*) provided crash rescue, and snow removal support." Peter wonders, "Without them we probably could not afford the airport."

Peter and lots of people of foresight, made it happen. Bangor International Airport plays a major role in air service, both civilian and military, today. It is a major contributor to the entire Eastern Maine economic structure. The University of Maine expanded to airport property, General Electric leased land and buildings for its turbine division and continues to provide some of the best jobs in the area today.

Peter says, "It took a lot of guts for a city of thirty-thousand people."

Bangor, Maine
Col John D'Errico and friend.
Vice Wing Commander, 101st Air
Refueling Wing, Me. ANG
Photo: "The Maineiac"

John came by his military career quite naturally. Peter says, "I had him around with me at the base." John remembers, "My first memory is of him standing there in a flight suit."

John was half way though college when, one day, he came to his dad and said, 'I'd like to fly.' Peter told him to apply for a pilot training slot with the National Guard. He says his dad told him, "Be an officer, and be a pilot; not a navigator."

John earned his commission from the ANG's Academy of Military Science in 1978. He got his pilot wings at Vance Air Force Base in 1979.

He's been flying ever since, during "Operation Desert Shield, Deny Flight, Restore Hope, Iraqi Freedom and Enduring Freedom."

He was Aircraft Commander on the first KC-135's, to support fighters, overhead in both New York and the Pentagon on September 11, 2001.

Colonel John D'Errico became Vice Commander of the 101st Air Refueling Wing of the Maine Air National Guard in June of 2006.

Major Peter D'Errico and Colonel John D'Errico were featured on the front page of the Bangor Daily News on February 3rd, 2007, noting the 60 year anniversary of the Maine Air National Guard.
Photo: Courtesy Bangor Daily

VIETNAM

The "Cold War" is the real, collective, heading for the war in Vietnam, the Korean conflict, and most of the world's troubles, between 1947 and 1991.

It was a period of conflict, tension, and competition between the United State and the Soviet Union. China assumed a significant role on the side of the Soviets...spreading communism. The US was intent on containing communism...halting the spread.

It was a critically dangerous time for the world...almost a half century of military buildup, with each side amassing destructive force enough to remove the other from the earth, many times.

Korea, Vietnam and the acceleration of late 20th century troubles in the Persian Gulf were a result. "Proxy wars," some historians call them. The United States and its western allies on one side. The Soviet Union and/or the People's Republic of China on the other side. Wars fought under another's name, because the major players, especially the United States and the U.S.S.R. were not willing to fight each other directly.

US military advisors became involved in Vietnam as early as 1950. In 1956, U.S. advisors assumed full responsibility for training the South Vietnamese army.

Large numbers of American combat troops began to arrive in 1965. U.S. troop strength in Vietnam, exceeded five-hundred-thousand in 1968.

United States forces decisively won most major engagements, they were in. It's inaccurate to say the United States lost the shooting war. The United States lost the propaganda war.

Most U.S. troops were withdrawn from Vietnam, following a peace accord, two years before South Vietnamese troops surrendered, on April 30, 1975. The U.S. had continued to support the South Vietnamese Army, mostly in the air and across the border in Cambodia and Laos.

Possibly, probably, the greatest influence on the outcome of the war, as far as the United States was concerned; it was the first war covered world wide on television. We had read the magazines, our newspapers and watched the "Movietone" news reels during earlier wars. We had never

Chocolate Mountain live fire range, north of Yuma, Arizona.
Russ Treadwell was on a weapons training deployment, transitioning
from the A-4E to the A-4M. The rocket is a five inch ZUNI.
Photo: Courtesy Russ Treadwell

November 1962. A second barrier along the "Berlin Wall" was under
construction, the United States had failed at the "Bay of Pigs," President
Kennedy was about to draw a line in the sand to stop a communist
victory in Vietnam. Another failure by the United States, to stop
communist expansion, was not tolerable.

At that point, most Americans probably couldn't find Vietnam on a map.
Russ Treadwell could. He was there already...off shore. Russ had
transferred to the 1st Battalion, 9th Marines at Camp Pendleton,
California....a special landing force, for quick response in the
southwestern Pacific. The unit spent a lot time at Camp Hanson,
Okinawa. "While I was in Okinawa, with that infantry battalion, we
floated around of the coast of Vietnam for half of that year."

Three years later, he would go back, in country, with Marine Attack
Squadron 121 the "Green Knights." "Probably the hairiest flying all the
time I was in the military, other than carrier operations, was flying those
tactical air coordination missions."

It started the month he arrived. "It was getting dark. The weather wasn't
very good." November 26, 1967, "Got a call. Marines were pinned
down. They needed help." Controllers directed him to the location.
Russ was flying an "A-4" jet, the same plane the "Blue Angels" used for
several years. "I rolled in and dropped napalm. We used the fire from
the napalm to adjust." The enemy force was entrenched in villages on
three sides of the Marines.

The citation awarding Russ Treadwell the "Distinguished Flying Cross" reads in part:

 "Despite poor visibility, Major Treadwell pinpointed the target and commenced his attack, immediately coming under intense automatic weapons fire. With complete disregard for his own safety, he skillfully maneuvered through the hostile fire on seven separate bombing and strafing runs and delivered all his ordnance with devastating effectiveness, silencing the enemy weapons and enabling the Marines to evacuate their casualties."

That's the way things were all the time he was in Vietnam, including a second tour, when he was awarded the "Air Medal."

Russ flew tactical Air Coordination Missions out of Da Nang. April 11, 1968, "We didn't find any targets. We were headed back." His flight leader's plane got hit. The pilot and observer ejected. "I watched them come down," about five hundred meters from a North Vietnamese village."

"The bad guys started coming across the rice paddy. Some of them were on water buffalos. I put down some 20 millimeter across the rice paddy. You couldn't shoot at them without clearance." They kept coming.

"The next time, I made a real low pass...the guy in the back seat said 'He could see the buffalo's eyes when we went by.' It scared the water buffalo. The buffalos took off and headed back for the village. The rest of um decided they better maybe not go over there."

His fuel was about gone but he waited for the chopper to pick the two guys up. "Just barely made it back to Da Nang. I don't think I had four minutes of fuel left when I landed."

Russ went back to Cherry Point, North Carolina when he came home. He trained replacement pilots, to get them ready for "Nam." He flew the TA-4F. In a competition between squadron instructors, Russ earned the "Top Gun" award. "That was some of the most satisfying flying that I did." Fun too. "It was big time fun!"

Knowlen flew the Ch-47 Chinook mostly, during his second tour in Nam. He was back in the central highlands again. "A lot of what we did was move the artillery around." The Chinook was large enough to carry thirty-two men. He moved troops a lot.

Chuck spent three years in Germany in the 70's. He commanded a seven hundred man Mechanized Infantry Battalion. "Best assignment I had," Chuck told me.

3d Battalion (Bayonets)
36th Infantry Regiment

The Officers and Men
of the
3d Battalion, 36th Infantry Regiment
cordially invite you to attend
a Change of Command Ceremony
on Friday, 13 December 1974, at 1400 hours
at the
Ayers Kaserne Parade Field
LTC CHARLES B. KNOWLEN
will assume command from
LTC EDWARD F. RHODES
A reception for LTC Knowlen
follows at the Ayers Officers' Club

Chuck Knowlen and his wife Beverly
December 13, 1974 at "Change of Command" ceremonies, as Chuck assumed command of 3rd Battallion, 36th Infantry Regiment.
The invitation is at the right.
Courtesy, Chuck Knowlen

Some bad memories in his twenty years and twenty days, but lots of good ones too, "It's the greatest experience. Obviously the two years in Vietnam were not pleasant. I was separated from my family quite a period of time, but I saw a lot of the world. I had some wonderful experiences. I had some really good assignments."

"People ask me why I retired after just twenty years." His answer is quick. "I tell them I had the best assignments in the Army, Command of an Infantry Battalion, and I probably would have had more advancement, but my family meant more to me. I wanted my two girls to spend four years in one high school. Maine was a better place to raise children than Washington, D.C."

44

Charles B Knowlen, Lt. Col. US Army Ret.
Greets the troops, volunteers at the Cole
Museum and works in his daughter's
greenhouse today. He said his golf is not
worth mentioning.
Photo: Courtesy Chuck Knowlen

His parting comment was true to character from Charles B. Knowlen,
Maine War Hero. "I don't think we went through anything worse than or
as bad as World War Two. I tell you what, those guys, I got great
respect for."

I'm quite sure they have the same respect for what you did too, Chuck.
We all do.

In spite of that and specific instructions from his doctors, "Don't engage in any strenuous activity." He's Chaplain for the police and fire departments in Greenville…just became a "Certified Chaplain" through the Maine Criminal Justice Academy. Police Chief Duane Alexander says, "Father Rob is a great guy! He's a real asset to our department," and said Alexander, "He's become a real friend."

Father Rob is also Chaplain for Charles A Dean Memorial Hospital, and occasionally helps police and fire department members with a little legal advice. He still has his license to practice law.

"We all think Father Rob is pretty great," Greenville Town Manager John Simko told me. "We're proud to have him in our community."

I got the impression, a lot of days are pretty tough for Father Rob, but I didn't hear a single word of bitterness or even disappointment. Even for a man of God, that's extraordinary.

As we parted, "Hang in there," he said.

He sure is!

JOHN W. WALLACE

Limestone, Maine

U.S. Army....July 1967 – July 1969

Sergeant, Airmobile

"There were a lot of worse days."

In a pack of angry dogs, he would be the Rottweiler. John Wallace is tough, determined and no-nonsense. "Being in war has made me realize life is too short...and life is definitely too short to be political." John is the President of the Maine State Council, Vietnam Veterans of America. He's a veteran's advocate, and he's good at it. "We need to take care of our vets today...not twenty years down the road!"

John had to be tough. He grew up on the streets of New York City. "I was big enough to stay out of the gangs. I had to be focused and I was strong enough to kick the hell out of the gang leader." He wanted to be a history teacher when he was growing up. "The Vietnam War changed that completely."

"I actually went down to enlist in the Navy. My whole family was Navy. They had a four year waiting list at the time, so I said I'll let them draft me for two years." They did, and the Army got him.

Sgt. John Wallace on a mountain top in Vietnam, 1968. The guys on the street in New York said, John was "A volcano ready to erupt at any time."
Photo; Courtesy John Wallace

They cut enough trees and limbs, a chopper managed to hover low enough to pick them up. "When I got on the chopper; that's when I realized I had busted my M-16." When they got back to base and he jumped off, "I went to the ground." He had twisted his right leg. "I didn't know it."

Adrenaline took care of the hurt while he was in battle. Back at base the medics took over, "Got all taped up...took some pain killers," and headed out on his next mission.

All in a days work when you're in combat. "There were a lot of worse days!"

John received the "Army Commendation medal with "V" for valor for his courageous action in Nam. He also got the "Bronze Star" and an "Air Medal."

Then he came home. "I got spit upon...called a baby killer."

Trouble started on the plane. "This 'hippy' type comes and sits next to me." John says, "I was being quiet." The guy looked over at him, "He looks at me and says you're a baby killer." The guy from the streets of New York took over.

The flight crew separated them and took John to the cockpit. "I got drunk on them, listening to Korean War stories, all the way to Kennedy Airport." There was a limousine waiting, as the pilot let him off at the end of the runway. He rode home in the limo, along with lots of horrible memories.

John is one hundred percent disabled today because of "Post Traumatic Stress Disorder," but thanks to a social worker at the Veteran's Administration, it's under control, and he's still bailing his fellow vets out of tough spots as a result.

'The only way you're going to handle the "PTSD" is to be the squad leader you were in Vietnam,' the social worker told him. 'Start advocating for veterans in Maine.' He hit the ground running, and he hasn't stopped since.

Memories of Vietnam return, now and then, "When I'm quiet," but he stays busy. No room for quiet times, and those memories. He travels thousands of miles each year, fighting battles for his fellow vets.

Governor John Baldacci made him his "Aide-d-Camp." That's a Colonel in the National Guard, and he serves on a bunch of other veteran committees. No time for quiet time...just the way he wants it.

What advice does he have for young people who are thinking of going into the military? "Go in the Air Force."

Caribou, Veteran's Day 2006
John Wallace, President, Chapter 478 and President,
Maine State Council Vietnam Veterans of America, Inc.
Photo: Courtesy John Wallace

VIETNAM MEMORIAL

Vietnam Monument and Memorial - Bangor, Maine
(Located at the Cole Land Transportation Museum)

The soldier with the rifle is modeled in the image of Eric
Wardwell of Orland. Eric and his entire squad of Marines were
killed in a mortar attack September 4, 1967 in Vietnam.
The "Huey" helicopter flew during the Vietnam War until it
crash landed in January of 1970. Pilot Tom Stryker and the
crew survived.

Photo: Cole Land Transportation Museum

JOHN HENRY CASHWELL, III

Bangor, Maine

U.S. Army........July 4, 1966 – December 1969
Retired from National Guard in 1995

CWO-4, Helicopter Pilot

"Someone else is going to die. You're never going to die."

This book is about heroes......it's about people who put their life on the line for their country. John Cashwell is a hero's hero. He was a helicopter pilot in Vietnam, and a damn good one. He has two "Silver Stars" a "Distinguished Flying Cross" several flying comrades, and a lot of G.I.s, he bailed out on the ground, who are still alive today, to prove it.

John grew up in New Hampshire....Derry and Portsmouth. He moved to Calais in 1979 because he would be around choppers. Flying has been a passion for him since long before he graduated from high school. He says he gave up an appointment to the Naval Academy, "because they couldn't guarantee me that I'd go to flight school, and I went off and joined the Army." When he started Army basic training, he had orders for "Basic Training en Route to Flight School."

JOHN   HENRY CASHWELL III.
The nametag does say "Nichols," John's adopted name. After the war, he officially changed his name back to his birth name: John Henry Cashwell, III.
Photo: Courtesy John Cashwell

59

He was just nineteen years old when he arrived in Saigon on August 24th, 1967. "There's no question that you're going to war, but no-one knows what war is until you get there. At age nineteen, you can't even imagine what you're going to do."

John was assigned to; 9th Aviation Battalion, 9th Infantry Division......flying "hash and trash" when he first arrived in "Nam." He flew Huey helicopters to deliver food and ammunition to guys in the field. "That's where you really start to learn how to fly, because you had to get in and out of places."

They flew at night.....there were no night goggles......fifteen hundred feet above small arms fire. The "hash and trash" choppers had only minimal protection. "I'm nineteen....I'm getting shot at and all you do is run, because there's no protection."

In November he was moved to co-pilot of a wing gunship; part of a "light fire team." John was in the chopper that flew about a half mile behind and to the side of the flight leader. By Thanksgiving, John was flight leader. The two pilots of the lead chopper of his team were burned when their helicopter crashed and flipped over. John pulled them out of the burning wreckage. Both survived. John earned a "Soldiers Medal" for his action that day.

For the rest of his two tours in Vietnam, he flew gun ships. "There are people whispering or screaming on the radio..... 'we're about to get compromised and killed here.' My job is to get these guys out of trouble." The helicopters were almost always under heavy fire. Historians say the chopper pilots in Vietnam were the most selfless people in the military. John says his mission was clear. "First is to save them and secondarily you're there to survive......but save them first.....survival comes with it........or it doesn't."

Many pilots didn't survive. "We'd go back and we'd have an empty mug....just like 'Twelve O'clock High." (*A 1949 movie starring Gregory Peck about Air Force flight crews that flew against Germany during WW II)* They talked to the lost pilot, as though he were still there.......scold him for messing up....praise him too....telling him how much they'll miss him; always remembering, "Someone else is going to die." Always believing, "You're never going to."

Vietnam 1968: More that 2,200 helicopter pilots were killed during the Vietnam War.

Photo: Courtesy John Cashwell

John says combat only got to him once. Ironically it was the last flight on his first hitch in Vietnam.

He was heading out on a mission when he noticed stuff going on near bunkers on a tree line. "I can't let it go you know." He got on the radio. "I said what's going on." A desperate voice came back. "We got four GIs pinned down.... 50 meters from the bunkers. Bad guys in bunkers along the tree line. The four guys.....the point men were pinned in a rice paddy, and no one to pick um up." They were between the enemy gunners and the main group of their unit.

John says, "I'm flying a gun ship. I got forty-eight rockets. I'm carrying all that weight. I have a full tank of gas." He had no business being there, he says. He asked his crew, "This is real stupid. We're going to do something real stupid. Now anybody here on this plane can say, we don't think we should do it, because it's that stupid." "You're going, we're going," they said.

The chopper was under heavy fire as John brought it in and landed about 45 yards from the bunker. "The four guys were right there on the ground under my chin bubble. The bastards wouldn't even get up." They were too scared.

His door gunners jumped out to get them. "They're getting shot at. I'm getting shot at and you're just sitting there with nothing but a Plexiglas windshield between you and the machine guns."

Gary Taylor who was a crew chief and door gunner on the chopper told me, "It always amazed me that John landed as close to that bunker as he did, facing it with no protection what-so-ever." Gary's one of the two who jumped out and got the guys.

It still wasn't over. With the guys on the skids, they had to fly several miles at night to a safe airfield. The helicopter was out of balance. Cashwell brought his choppers in as slow as he could, probably still twenty-five miles an hour, and as low as he could.... probably four or five feet above the runway. He had too much weight on the nose to hover. He opened his canopy and yelled to the guys on the skids, you have to jump. They jumped. They survived. John received the "Distinguished Flying Cross" for his action that day.

Distinguished Flying Cross Awarded for heroism or extraordinary achievement while participating in aerial flight. Photo: Dept. of Defense

Bill Anderson says, "He definitely put his life and the co-pilot's life at risk.....it was pretty special."

The things Anderson and his guys did for their country was pretty special too. He received the "Silver Star," three "Bronze Stars," and a "Purple Heart" for his action in Nam. Still he says, "If it were not for John and guys like him, there's no way I'd be here talking to you."

On another occasion Lt. Anderson and seven Rangers were being inserted to attack a Viet Cong battalion headquarters. The chopper that attempted to drop them was shot up trying to land. The Huey flew a short distance to a safe landing zone unable to fly any farther.

After shooting up the tree line, where the enemy headquarters was located, John and his wingman Bob Schultz picked up the patrol and insert them at the tree line. The rangers finished off the headquarters.

John and Bob went back to pick them up after the successful attack. That meant more trouble. The unexpected passengers added too much weight to the choppers, to get off the rice paddy without losing power. Landing with them was easier than taking them out. John started bouncing his chopper along the ground, but with the weight of the armament, fuel and the rangers; they didn't know if they could get out of the small clearing.

The tree line at the end of the rice paddy was getting close and they weren't going to make it; until John's lead ship bounced squarely on a

Vietnamese "hooch" (*a small Vietnamese shelter*) flattening it, and giving him momentum and power enough to clear the trees. The flattened hooch provided room enough for Schultz to follow through the tree line where the hooch was just standing.

The day was filed away in memory until one day, well after the war, just a few years ago; a friend put John on the telephone. For a long moment the man on the other end couldn't talk. "Do I know you?" John asked. 'You have saved my life a thousand times.' Bill Anderson said. 'I was one of the men on your skids that day.'

John says he was overcome. When I interviewed him, there was a very long silence before he could even tell me about it. Anderson too, had to pause several times, to get his emotions in check, when I spoke with him.

I'd like to report, that after dangling his life, so precariously so many times, John Cashwell came home to a heroes welcome, but he didn't. "Baby Killer!...or worse" That's what he heard, like so many other people who put it on the line in Vietnam.

Even when he tried to celebrate and take a date to the "Top of the Mark" restaurant in San Francisco, John was denied admission. He was still twenty years old. This guy who had done so much, under the most extreme conditions, wasn't old enough to get into the restaurant. "I went and bought a bottle of wine off a wino and sat on some steps up in the middle of San Francisco with my date, drinking out of a bottle of wine in a paper bag."

He did go back to school after he returned, but he kind of tuned out of society for a few years. "The first thing I did when I got back was to grow hair as fast as I can, anywhere I could grow it so that I didn't look like a military guy." It was several years before he told anyone what he had done.

Bangor, Maine 2006
John Cashwell at Seven Islands Land Company, Maine headquarters.
Photo: Don Colson

Phouc Vinh, Vietnam
Base camp for the 28th
Infantry.
Photo: US Army

"As a group, we didn't spend much time there." A few days, "We'd come back and get cleaned up and wait for a new assignment." Three or four days later they were dropped off in the jungle again... ambush patrols. The Army took away the rifle and gave Ed a grenade launcher.

In November of 1966, the 28th, the "Black Lions" participated in "Operation Attleboro," reinforcing the 25th Infantry. In a twenty day series of battles, US forces stopped the Viet Cong from taking strategic positions northwest of Saigon. It's estimated that upwards of fifty thousand troops were involved in the battles.

As the 28th pushed the Viet Cong back at Ap Cha Do, the largest battle of the operation, they discovered a base camp that stretched for over a mile in the thick jungle, and a large cache of ammo. There were 19,000 grenades, 1,135 pounds of explosives, 400 bangalore torpedoes, and a command radio system; and there were 399 Viet Cong bodies. The 28th Infantry received the "Presidential Unit Citation" for extraordinary heroism in the battle of Ap Cha Do.

Army, Presidential Unit Citation is awarded for extraordinary heroism in action against an armed enemy.

The year in Vietnam was like that for Ed. "I was at the front the whole twelve months."

January; Operation Cedar Falls...the invasion of the Iron Triangle was next. During that, the 28th discovered the largest enemy hospital found during the war.

Operation Tucson in February.

Operation Junction City followed. The Army took away the grenade launcher and gave Ed a machine gun.

Then Operation Billings, a big one. Twenty Two American battalions with an Army of Vietnam troops.

A tough year, "In my case it was the stress." he says.

September; Operation Shenandoah....Search and destroy ops... daily contact with the "VC" and booby traps. "We were counting down the days." They captured 84 tons of rice and destroyed seventeen large Viet Cong camps.

Ed remembers his last days in Nam. "I just came off ambush patrol," in from the jungle for the last time...going home. "The Ninth North Vietnamese Army opened fire on the base." Five hundred enemy troops were killed...twenty-five American guys died.

January 1967
Ed Leonard in the Vietnamese jungle, The "Iron Triangle."
Photo: Courtesy Ed Leonard

Later that month, battle weary, carrying stress, even he didn't recognize, Ed boarded the chopper that would take him out of there. "We were flying along the tree tops...this machine gunner opened up with his machine gun. Here, we thought we were all safe. All of a sudden we thought we were being fired on." Nope. It was a joke. Just the chopper guys giving them one last scare. "I won't forget it."

Five months after he returned from "Nam" Ed got out of the Army, exactly two years from the day he went in. His old employer had kept his job open for him. "At first I was pretty good," until he was passed over for promotion. The boss said he hadn't been there long enough. Ed thought the time he was away should be counted. He got angry and quit. The first real sign of trouble. He still didn't see it.

He became a distributor for Pepperidge Farm. That went well, until the larger stores made more demands. "My anger grew worse." He quit that. "I just stopped working for eighteen months."

Things got so bad at home, his wife, "She almost walked out on me," until the day the Veteran's Center in Bangor called. "Where's Ed?" Apparently, "At a parade down town I signed something."

It took him a while, but finally he worked up the courage to try the Vet's Center. "That's when I found out I had "Post Traumatic Stress Disorder." It was an important day for him. Treatments, counseling sessions, which he still attends, put him on the long road back. Today, "I can lead a very good life, as long as I take my medicine, and pay attention to what I'm suppose to be doing.

The Army is not all bad memories for that quiet boy from Hermon. "Being from a poor family I never dreamed of landing in Alaska, Japan, Guam or even California on my way home." R & R in Hawaii wasn't so bad either. "It was a dream place."

What's he say about his military service today?" "Although the majority of us were draftees, when it came to combat we did our duty with honor and it made us better men."

Edward Leonard, January 2007, Age 64
Photo: Courtesy Ed Leonard

ALEXANDER "SANDY" STYMIEST

Brewer, Maine

U.S. Air Force (and A.N.G.).........October 1947 – April 1, 1980

Major, Fighter Pilot

"I've had the F-106 up above 70,000...that's really up there."

Sandy Stymiest is a fighter pilot. He's a likable guy.....easy to talk to. He exemplifies the unique confidence of a guy who's flown a plane twice the speed of sound. Anyone who's been in the military knows what I'm talking about; fighter pilots are in an exclusive fraternity.

Sandy's another of the guys who got their start a little early. He's a Brewer boy who enlisted in Maine Air National Guard when he was just sixteen years old. "I wasn't supposed to be there, but I was."

He spent his early years in the enlisted ranks as a radio mechanic. His National Guard unit was activated in 1951, about a year after the Korean War began. He didn't go to Korea. Part of Sandy's unit served at Dow Air Force Base in Bangor. Sandy was one of four or five people assigned to the Air Force Base at Presque Isle. "My particular job....they needed me up there." Sandy worked on the radios in F-86 "Sabre" jets. There were three F-86 squadrons in Presque Isle, prepared to defend the country. (*Presque Isle Air Force Base was closed in 1962. Dow Air Force Base closed in 1968.*)

Sandy had made it up to Staff Sergeant, but he got out of the Air Force just before the end of the Korean War. He wasn't out long. July 1953; "The Air National Guard was requested from the Air Force to send them pilots.....I volunteered to go."

Officer Candidate School and pilot training behind him, Sandy returned to the Maine Air National Guard again as a pilot in the 101st Fighter Interceptor wing in Bangor. He flew F-94's. Sandy stayed with the Guard until October 1962 when he again returned to active duty. Once again the Air Force needed pilots.

Sandy was flight commander of a wing of F-100s at Cannon Air Force Base at Clovis, New Mexico, first. He was transferred to the 20th Tactical Fighter Wing at Weathersfield AFB in England. The 20th rotated between Weathersfield and Chili AFB at Ishmir, Turkey and Aviano AFB in Northern Italy. "We stood nuclear alert." It was the "Cold War" and the Soviets and the US were staring each other down across the threat of nuclear annihilation. Sandy says if the call came, "We knew exactly where we were going." Soviet Union? "Oh yeah."

1967: Phan Rhang Vietnam
Alexander " Sandy Stymiest with his F-100
Photo: Courtesy Sandy Stymiest

Next stop, Vietnam, "to fly close air support of troops on the ground." He was assigned to the 35th Tactical Fighter Wing at Phan Rhang, about 25 miles south of Camron Bay, flying the F-100 "Super Sabre." "If the Army had gotten themselves in a crack, they would call in for air support, right now." The fighters would try to bail them out.

F-100 Super Sabre of the 35th Tactical Fighter Wing.
Photo: US Air Force

The jets had bigger guns, 20 MM, and bombs, which the choppers didn't have. The jets would scream in, guns blasting, at 400 knots, many times fifteen or twenty feet above the ground.

Sandy will never forget one day, "A radar site was being overrun. These guys were up on a mountain and they were being over run by the bad guys. We were in the clouds at 700 feet....we had the good guys on one side of a dirt road, and the bad guys on the other side of a dirt road. We had to go in and strafe those bad buys with a 20 MM and not hit the good guys." The jets pulled away and jettisoned their bombs and napalm so they could get in faster. Six US guys died before the jets hit the enemy troops, that day....the rest were saved.

Sandy's first assignment was at Loring Air Force Base in Northern Maine, after he returned from Vietnam. "I met a T/Sgt that was working in the office and we got talking and he was one of the people that survived that overrun." He doesn't remember the Sergeant's name, but he knows he saved at least one life during his time over there.

Sandy received the "Distinguished Flying Cross" for his action that day. During the time he was in Vietnam, he received nine air medals and the Vietnamese Cross of Gallantry.

He flew six different fighters during his thirty years in the Air Force.... F-84, F-94, F-89, F-100, F-106, and the F-4. The F-106 and the F-4 both fly at twice the speed of sound. How is it possible to react that fast to fly those planes? "You gotta be way ahead of it, because if you ever get behind the curve, then you're in trouble. I've had the F-106 up above 70,000 feet a number of times.....that's really up there."

F-106 Delta Dart

December 1959: the F-106 set a world speed record of 1,525.96 MPH
Photo: US Air Force

He was promoted to Captain, out of that assignment. "Went to Assistant Chief of Staff for Operations, at 2nd Fleet, for a three star Admiral." He was back on board....the Mt Whitney...the flag ship.

Tom, still a Captain, was made Assistant Chief of Staff for "Fleet Tactical Deception Group Atlantic." "That's the deception guys for the Atlantic Fleet. They do all the electronic surveillance and jamming, and things like that." Highly classified stuff.

He was awarded the "Legion of Merit" for his service there: **"An extremely perceptive and resourceful leader, Captain Kelly exercised an innate ability to assimilate the multi-faceted aspects of naval operations within both the North Atlantic Treaty Organization and U.S. National arenas so as to ensure the most appropriate assets were available to meet widely diverse operational requirements."**

Legion of Merit

Tom Kelly III, 1973. The day he took command of the USS John King (DDG-3) Photo: Courtesy Tom Kelly

He joined forces with four other retired Captains after he retired. They formed a trading company. "Kelstar International" dealt in everything from electronic warfare, for the Department of Defense, to Hershey bars.

He did that for a year and a half...got a call, one day, from a friend, a native of Bar Harbor, who was living in Saudi Arabia. "He told me the Saudis had never seen a Pepsi machine which dispenses juices." He gave Tom the name of a man in Riyadh who had the largest catering company in Saudi Arabia and one of the largest in the world. "One thing led to another, and I ended up over in Saudi Arabia."

Tom made arrangements with a California company, which made Pepsi machines, and the largest juice 'bag in a box' distributor on the east coast, "I linked those two together."

He set up a company, "Just Juice," hired "hundreds of guys," and had three distribution points in Saudi Arabia. "I lived over there for four years." The company was worth several million dollars by 1997.

Back home, in Brewer, his mother was taken ill. "I said I'm not going to put my mother in a nursing home." He came home; bought a home in Blue Hill, and with his sister Nonnie, helped take care of his mother. She passed away in 1999.

Life settled down on Woods Pond in Blue Hill, for a while. Tom's wife, Laurie (Nichols), a Bangor native, knew it wouldn't last. In May of 2005, she told "The Ellsworth American," "Tom is such a patriotic person, and I know how much it means to him to be there, helping out." "If they told him to go over and clean toilets," she said, "he'd be there." Tom says he's "Fortunate to have strong support from Laurie."

Tom was back, in Iraq in 2005, at "Camp Victory," ground zero for the war. Home was a cramped trailer, surrounded by razor wire. He was working with the same man from Saudi Arabia, "He had the contract to feed the American troops. After the explosion at Mosul DAFC (*dining facility*) he asked me to do what I could to tighten up security at all DFACs in Iraq."

At first, Laurie didn't know. Tom says, "I'm sitting over in Baghdad in Saddam's palace. I'm getting my picture taken, sitting on this great big, golden, throne." He laughs. "And I sent the picture back to my wife. Boy did I catch hell." Laurie thought Tom was at the company headquarters in Kuwait.

Tom told "The Ellsworth American, "I'm not there for the money. I could make as much money working for the Department of Transportation, as I do over in Iraq. I'm there to do whatever I can to support these young soldiers; both our soldiers and these young Iraqi Army and National Guard soldiers, who more and more are on the front lines."

a Professor at the University of Maine, who would become his wife. In 1974 when he retired, Maine is where they settled.

Chuck spent the twenty years, after he retired from the Air Force, with the Postal Service. He retired from there in 1996.

Today he's a volunteer fire fighter for the town of Dedham and monitors water quality of Phillips Lake for the town. He also volunteers at the Cole Museum.

He has a commercial pilot's license and even owned and flew a homebuilt plane for a few years. Still stinging, just a little, that he didn't get to sit in the front seat of those Air Force jets. "The only thing was wrong was if I could have just got into that doggoned pilot's training."

In spite of that, he's a big advocate of military service. "I believe in it. It's one of the best places to be. It's a super place to travel and learn. I tell you I wouldn't have missed it for anything."

Charles and Valerie McClead, 1983.
Photo: Courtesy the McCleads

CLAIR BEMIS

Levant, Maine

U.S. Marines..............May 1953 – May 1973

Gunnery Sergeant

"They had both been hit. They didn't hardly get their feet on the ground."

Clair Bemis served a tour of duty in Korea, and two tours in Vietnam, during his twenty years in the Marines. In spite of all the action he saw, and he did see a lot, he's happy he did it. He says, he's very proud of his service. "I'll put my uniform on and walk right down the street in a minute."

Clair got an early start...enlisting on May 28, 1953, his 17th birthday. "I wasn't a good student. I hated school and er....I went in the Marine Corps. and they sent me to school."

He is the forth member of his family to serve in the Marines.

Clair was a member of the "Pine Tree Platoon" in basic training. Every member was from the state of Maine.

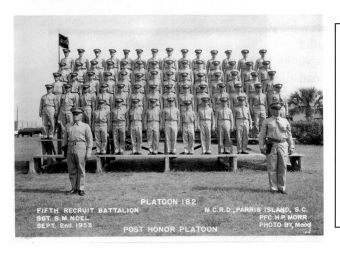

Parris Island, S.C., September 1953

The Maine platoon, (Post Honor Platoon) Every member was from the state of Maine.
Photo: U.S. Marines

107

Bangor, Maine:
At the Cole Land Transportation Museum: Clair's in the middle, talking about the history of the old Enfield Railroad Station with a couple from Michigan.
Photo: Don Colson

Clair says the vet's have benefited too. "We buried some thoughts that we couldn't bring out, but this has made us bring um out, and now we can face um better."

RICHARD E. GIFFARD

Brewer, Maine

U.S. Army......................October 31, 1952 – August 1, 1980

Sergeant Major, Infantry

"She sat her in my son's lap. He lit up like a Christmas tree."

Dick Giffard got out of the army after his first hitch. That lasted fifty-seven days. "I realized that was my calling," he says. For a total of twenty-eight-years, the army was the calling for Dick and his wife Barbara.

"Wives are at least half the equation.....maybe more." he says. "They never know when you go to work, when you're going to get home. My wife was the doctor, the lawyer, the indian chief, the teacher, the coach, the minister........she did everything." Dick made sure he had Barbara's approval. She approved. He reenlisted.

Dick Giffard was a Brewer boy.....was and is. He remembers when his dad was the neighborhood "Air-Raid" warden during WW II. He remembers the watchtower that stood where the Dunkin Donuts shop is now. Volunteer observers manned the tower, twenty-four hours a day, watching for enemy planes, if they should come. I don't believe any ever did. We were lucky.

Dick was a pretty good ball player at Brewer High School....football, basketball and baseball. Later on he got to play football, on the base team at Fort Dix, with several pros, including a man by the name of Roosevelt Grier. Grier's one of the better ones the New York Giants ever had. A catcher by the name of Roseboro was one of the better ones the Dodgers ever had too. Dick played on a baseball team against him, in Germany.

Dick was drafted into the military. The Korean War was on. He was one of only ten, from his company in basic training, who didn't get sent there immediately. Instead of Korea, Dick became an "M-1" rifle instructor. "Because I was a hunter, and I was from Maine, and they liked the way I handled my weapon." He spent so much time on the range.... "That's why my hearing's not worth a damn today." No earplugs back then.

Korea 1965
Dick Giffard on the DMZ.
Photo: Courtesy Dick Giffard

Dick did get to Korea after the war. He was on the DMZ. (*The Demilitarized Zone is the two-mile wide, one-hundred-and-fifty-one mile long, hunk of territory that has separated North and South Korea since the war.*) Infiltrators were still trying to sneak across the DMZ Dick says, "We used to have firefights ever once in a while."

There were two tours in Vietnam for him. He was with the 101st Air Mobile the first time he was there, in 1968. He was battalion sergeant in charge of a "Tactical Operations Center." His team built, manned and moved the TACs as the battles moved. TACs were communications centers and often well buried. Each time Dick's team had to call in a dozer and dig a new hole, about twelve by twenty-four, and cover it with big metal panels, called P.S.P., covered by a blimp skin (*rubber*) and several layers of sand bags.

Vietnam
Sgt Richard Giffard during his second tour in Vietnam.
Photo: Courtesy Dick Giffard

In June of 1969, he was wounded during a mortar attack at a fire base in North Vietnam. He didn't even know it until the rest of the wounded men were evacuated. As the last chopper was leaving, his commander told Dick he had better get aboard. That's when he discovered blood running down his face, and all over one leg.

112

The citation for the "Bronze Star" Medal with "V" device (*first Oak Leaf Cluster*) reads in part:

"For heroism while participating in ground combat on June 1969, Master Sergeant Giffard distinguished himself. During the initial attack, several men, including Sergeant Giffard, were wounded. Sergeant Giffard, with complete disregard for his own personal safety, moved throughout the area, under the intense mortar fire, in order to reach the more seriously wounded and pull them to safety."

DEPARTMENT OF THE ARMY
Headquarters 101st Airborne Division (Airmobile)
APO San Francisco 96383

GENERAL ORDERS
NUMBER 10935
21 August 1969

AWARD OF THE BRONZE STAR MEDAL WITH "V" DEVICE (FIRST OAK LEAF CLUSTER)

1. TC 320. The following AWARD is announced.

GIFFARD, RICHARD E 005-28-7626 MASTER SERGEANT Headquarters and Headquarters Company 2d Battalion 327th Infantry APO San Francisco 96383

Awarded: The Bronze Star Medal with "V" Device
Effective month: NA
Date action: 14 June 1969
Theater: Republic of Vietnam
Reason: For heroism while participating in ground combat on 14 June 1969, Master Sergeant Giffard distinguished himself while serving as Operations Sergeant with Headquarters and Headquarters Company, 2d Battalion, 327th Infantry at Fire Support Base Berchtesgaden, Republic of Vietnam. During the early morning hours on the cited date, an enemy force of unknown size launched an intense mortar and small arms attack on the fire base. During the initial attack, several men, including Sergeant Giffard, were wounded. Sergeant Giffard, with complete disregard for his own personal safety, moved throughout the area, under the intense mortar fire, in order to reach the more seriously wounded, and pull them to safety. After the wounded had been moved to a protected area, Sergeant Giffard again moved from the protected bunker and exposed himself to intense small arms and rocket propelled grenade fire to set up radio antennas and reestablish communications. Sergeant Giffard's outstanding courage and devotion to duty were in keeping with the highest traditions of the military service and reflect great credit upon himself, his unit, and the United States Army.
Authority: By direction of the President of the United States under provisions of Executive Order 11046.

FOR THE COMMANDER:

OFFICIAL:

HUGH A. MACDONALD
Colonel, GS
Chief of Staff

Joseph P. Hatch, Major
DATE H. HAYES

Department of the Army General Orders Number **10935**, awarding the "Bronze Star" To M/Sgt Richard Giffard

Even after he did that, Dick went back out, under fire, to set up radio antennas and reestablish communications.

Doctors removed the shrapnel from his head. He's still walking around with a piece of metal in his knee, today.

The second time in "Nam" he was there at the end.......there as the war ended. Remember the pictures of how tough things were around Saigon during those last days. That's where Dick was.

Hard to believe but regrettably, things were worse when he got back to the U.S. "Before we left Vietnam, they said when you land in San Francisco, take your uniform off, and put on civilian clothes. I said why in the hell am I doing that? I'm proud of my uniform. Well, a lot of people are causing problems when they see military people in the airports."

He changed his clothes. "I felt like I was sneaking into my own country. I went over there and put my life on the line and came back and had to sneak in, so nobody could see me. That's atrocious!" Dick says he still thinks about it today.

There's at least one more special chapter in the story of Dick Giffard......Dick and Barbara Giffard. The army has a part in that too.

Mid 1950's......their career was going well, but they wanted children. They decided to adopt. A tangle of bureaucratic red tape stood in their way in the U.S. Officials in New Jersey, where they were stationed, told them to adopt in Maine, their home state. Back home, Maine officials tried to send them back to New Jersey.

Dick threw his hands up.....called his battalion commander and asked to be transferred back to Germany. When he explained why, the transfer came through within days. 1959, their son Gary was adopted. He was about six months old when Barbara picked him up in Frankfurt.

Life was good, but a daughter.... a sister, would make things perfect. Once again they approached adoption officials.... this time in Alabama. Dick was a training sergeant at Fort Rucker. Weeks passed... months passed. The adoption representatives, and Dick and Barbara worried about how Gary would welcome a new sister. He was only five.

The call came in 1963. "Come to Montgomery."

Gary, Barbara & Shari, The Giffard family! (1965) They were writing a letter to Dick in Korea.
Photo: Courtesy the Giffards

Dick says, "They brought her in. The lady took her right to my son first. She sat her in my son's lap. He lit up like a Christmas tree." Gary's new sister Shari was an immediate hit.

Dick went right back to Eastern Fine Paper after he retired. That's where he was working when he was drafted in 1952.

The Giffards, all four, went back to Brewer to live.

Brewer, Maine – Late 1980s

Sergeant Major Richards Giffard spent the last five years of his military career as an ROTC instructor at the University of Maine. Photo: Courtesy Dick Giffard

VIETNAM WAR

Of the two-point-six-million Americans who served in the Vietnam War, between one and one-point-six-million, either fought in combat, provided close combat support, or were at least fairly regularly exposed to enemy attack.

The average age of the 58,249 killed in Vietnam was just under twenty-four years of age.

The average age of an infantryman fighting in Vietnam was nineteen years old.

Five men killed in Vietnam were sixteen years old.

7,484 women served in Vietnam. (6,250 were nurses.)

Eight women died...all were nurses. One, Sharon Ann Lane, died in combat.

KOREA

Some simply called the "Korean War," the "Cold War." In fact, war was never declared. The Korean "Conflict"..."Police Action"... "War," never officially ended.

From 1950 until 1953, the United States combined with United Nations forces; to take a stand against, what was believed, to be a worldwide threat to democratic nations everywhere.

After World War Two, the Korean Peninsula had been divided at the 38th parallel. The government in the north was backed by the Soviet Union. The United States backed the government in the south.

On June 25, 1950, war broke out. The North Korean Army attacked several strategic points along the parallel and headed south. The United Nations immediately condemned the attack.

Equipped by the Soviets, and backed by the Chinese, the North Koreans moved south, quickly. Within days, South Korean forces, outnumbered and out-gunned, were in full retreat.

The attack by the north came as a surprise in the United States. As late as June 20th, Secretary of State Dean Acheson told Congress, war was unlikely in Korea.

The first significant American combat unit to arrive in Korea was part of the U.S. Army's 24th Infantry Division, which had been based in Japan. On July 5th, 1950, it entered battle against the North Koreans at Osan.

Initially, the tide of battle looked grim, but the tide turned, as more troops and supplies arrived. United States and South Korean troops grabbed the opportunity, and landed far behind the North Korean lines at Incheon.

Seoul was retaken. The North Korean Army was almost cut off.

With ideas of uniting all of Korea, U.S. and U.N. forces continued to move north. That concerned the Chinese who feared they wouldn't stop at North Korea. In October the Chinese entered the war.

The tide began to see-saw again. Seoul fell…was recaptured.

The front stabilized by the middle of 1951. The war continued, but from that point on, little territory changed.

With the U.N.'s acceptance of an Indian proposal for a Korean armistice, a cease fire was established on July 27, 1953. The line was drawn, in the proximity of the 38th parallel. The demilitarized zone, along the 38th parallel, is still defended to this day, by North Korean troops on one side, and South Korean and American troops on the other.

> American casualties during the "Korean War"
> Battle deaths……………..…………33,741
> **Battle deaths – Maine…………….…..233**
> Other deaths …………………..…..20,557*
> Americans wounded……………..…103,284

*"Other deaths" Service members who died, but not as a result of combat.

LEWIS "RED" MILLETT

Mechanic Falls, Maine

U.S. Army............1937 – 1973

Colonel, Infantry (Medal of Honor reciepient.)

"I guess I was born to be a warrior."

Colonel Lewis Millett served in two armies, in three wars, on three continents. He was Court Martialed for desertion. He became an Army Colonel, and oh yes... he received the "Medal of Honor."

Osan Air Force Base, Korea: October 6, 1975
Retired Army Colonel Lewis Millett during a return visit to South Korea in 1975.
Photo: Stars and Stripes

He told me, "The next day I did it again, and then I got orders not to do it any more."

I asked him why he did it...what went through his mind to take such courageous but perilous action? "I'm a warrior. I never feel bad in battle. The only bad time is when I lost men."

President Harry Truman presented the "Medal of Honor" to Captain Lewis Millett of Mechanic Falls, Maine, on July 15, 1951.

Later in the Korean War, Millett was recognized for his aid in the rescue of a pilot, shot down behind enemy lines. His action in Korea, also earned him the Distinguished Service Cross, another "Silver Star" three "Bronze Stars with "V" device, four Purple Hearts, and a bottle of Scotch. That came from the 2nd South Africa Fighter Squadron for saving the downed pilot.

Hill 180, Osan, Korea 1975
Retired Army Col. Lewis Millett points to the area where he led the bayonet charge on February 7, 1951.
Photo: Stars & Stripes

Not done yet......Colonel Millett spent five and a half years in Southeast Asia during the Vietnam War. A lot of that time was in classified assignments, so we don't know what he did there. I think we have an idea. He refused all decorations for his action in Vietnam, saying he wasn't there for recognition, but to provide freedom for people under attack by forces of tyranny.

Some of Colonel Millett's additional decorations include two Legions of Merit, two Air Medals, the French Croix de Guerre, the Canadian War Cross and the Vietnam Cross of Gallantry.

I asked him what the "Medal of Honor" has meant to him? "A lot of speeches," He said. The "Medal of Honor" Society made him lifetime "Sergeant of Arms." I got the impression, he's quite proud of that.

Colonel Lewis Millett
"A lot of Speeches."
Photo: Courtesy VFW Post#
10216 Song Si, So Korea

He served as Justice of the Peace in Merkel, Texas after he retired. He told Mike Rush of "Stars and Stripes, "I couldn't find a job, so I ran for election, and they elected me."

Colonel Millett married Winona Williams of Abilene, Texas. She passed away in December of 1993. They had four children...Lewis Jr., Timothy, Elizabeth and John. Staff Sergeant John Moreton Millett, their youngest son, was killed on December 12th, 1985 in a plane crash. He was serving with Task Force 502 in the Multinational Peacekeeping Force in Sinai.

Songtan Si, So. Korea
Colonel Lewis Millett at the "Hill 180-Bayonet Hill" Marker.

Photo: Stars & Stripes

Colonel Millett wrote a poem in memory of his son, and soldiers who have made the ultimate sacrifice:

"A Soldier's Prayer – by Col. Lewis L. Millett

I've fought when others feared to serve.
I've gone where many failed to go.
I've lost friends in war and strife, who valued duty
over the love of life.
I've shared the comradeship of pain.
I've searched these lands for men that we've lost.
I've sons who've served our land of liberty who'd
Fight to see that other lands are free.
I've seen the weak forsake humanity.
I've heard fakers praise our enemy.
I've seen challenged men stand even bolder.
I've seen the duty, the honor, the sacrifice of the
soldier.
Now I understand the meaning of all lives,
The lives of comrades of not so long ago.
So to you who answered duties siren call, may
God bless you my son, may God bless you all."

Lewis Millett turned 86 on December 15, 2006. His parting words to me as we ended our conversation, "God Bless America."

Some photos in this chapter: "Used with permission from the Stars & Stripes"

PAUL R. CURTIS

Bangor, Maine

U.S. Army...................October 17, 1952 – October, 1954

Corporal, Infantry

"I'm finally actually here in Korea......my mother is going to hate this!"

"I can still remember my first Army meal in the vast echoing mess hall at Ft. Meade (Maryland) – warm hot dogs, watery mashed potatoes, raw onion salad, and canned peaches." It's been over fifty years since that day for Paul Curtis.

Paul was a draftee in the Army. He wasn't married when he went in so, he says, he wrote regularly to his mother. That helps him remember many of the details of his military experience. His mother kept his letters.

Korea: 1953
Shortly after the ceasefire.

Cpl. Paul Curtis dressed for a parade, in honor of those who died at "Outpost Harry."

Photo: Courtesy Paul Curtis

Paul's never been able to understand why he ended up where he did in the Army. He says, "I had scored well on the scientific and professional test, and was led to believe this would put me in something like the medical area." He ended up in the infantry.....1st Battalion, Intelligence and Reconnaissance, of the 5th Regimental Combat Team, in Korea.

"We all knew that EUCOM (*European Command*) meant a relatively cushy assignment with occupational forces in Germany," while. FECOM (*Far-east Command*) meant Korea. From his platoon, two men with the last name of "Curtis" went in opposite directions. Tommy Curtis went to EUCOM. Paul Curtis went to the Korean War.

He remembers his first night there, too. He thought he was watching a whopper of a thunderstorm......"It suddenly dawned on me...that's not a storm, it's artillery, and that's the front line! I finally realized, I'm finally actually here in Korea." He knew, "My mother is going to hate this!"

Outpost Harry was on the mountain top, just to the right of center in the picture. You can see the artillery burst.
The defenders were told to "Hold at all Costs." Withdrawal was not an option.
The motto of the "Outpost Harry Survivors Association" is, "We Held!"
Photo: James Jarboe, Outpost Harry Survivors Association

The battle for "Outpost Harry" is one of Paul's most vivid memories. The outpost was on a hill just north of the front line in the Chorwon Valley region in central Korea. It was considered critical to the defense of the area. He says it was continuous bedlam, "From exploding artillery

126

and mortar rounds, Katyusha rockets from the Chinese side, machine gun and rifle fire. It was deafening and terrifying."

During the battle, Master Sergeant Ola Mize won a Medal of Honor. Paul's friend Bill Scott was badly wounded in the battle. He had been with Bill since they headed off to basic training together from Columbus, Ohio half a year before. He didn't see him again until he got home, after the war.

Paul, a corporal and a squad leader, says the signing of the truce agreement on July 27, 1953 is certainly among the highlights of the war for him.

His letters to his mother described the time.

July 20, 1953

"Dear Mom,

We are on line again, but in about the worst positions I ever saw. The country up here is much more mountainous than in central Korea. Our bunker leaks pretty badly, but is not too bad.....there are no roads within seven miles of this place."

July 27, 1953

"Dear Mom,

Well it looks like today is the big day everyone has been waiting for. I was helping build a bunker when we heard the news that the armistice had been signed at 10 this morning. The ceasefire is supposed to be at 10 tonight. We are hoping they (The Chinese) don't unload all their ammunition on us just before."

August 2, 1953

"Dear Mom,

The Chinese poured everything they had on us for an hour before the ceasefire, and we did the same to them.

Maine Korean War Memorial

Maine Korean War Memorial, Mt Hope Cemetery, Bangor, Maine

The names of the 245 Maine men, dead or missing in Korea, are engraved on the memorial.

It was dedicated on July 29, 1995, just two days after the national memorial was dedicated in Washington, D.C.

The flags of the twenty-two nations who participated in the United Nations force, line the walkway.

Photo: Ken Buckley, Burton-Goode-Sargeant Chapter 1, KWVA,

ALBERT GIBSON

Brewer, Maine

U.S.Army.................June 1951 – June 1955

Staff Sergeant, Forward Observer, Power Equipment Mechanic

"spending Christmas Eve under a tarp in 1952."

Al Gibson remembers the World War Two years clearly. His brother was in the Pacific. "I remember WW II as a young boy and following the war on the radio.....writing to my brother."

His dad ran an A & P store in New Jersey. "End of the week he'd bring the ration stamps back in the kitchen, sit at that big dining room table there, and paste um all in the books that he had to turn in to the government." Grocers had to provide proof that they only sold quantities that met the ration requirements.

Al got his turn, in the Korean War.

Technically, it wasn't a war. We never officially called it that. President Harry Truman called it a "Police Action" under the umbrella of the

Korea 1952
Al Gibson on the 38th Parallel.
Photo: Courtesy Al Gibson

United Nations. That way, he avoided a vote in the congress. It started on June 25, 1950, and the cease-fire was declared on July 27, 1953. Technically, the war has never officially ended. Our troops are still there.

There are lots of conflicting reports about casualties. Some official accounts say more than a million South Koreans were killed in the "police action" and over eleven percent of the North Korean population died. Our government is still arguing about the number of Americans who were killed in Korea. Initial reports put the number at 54,246.

December 29th, 1951, Al's unit climbed off another ship, at Inchon, Korea, to relieve the 1st Cavalry Division. "They had the stuffing kicked out of them by the Chinese. They needed to be relieved."

Al caught patrol duty soon after his arrival in Korea. "Patrols, patrols and more patrols!" he says. "Winter, cold, cold, cold. Twenty below on many occasions."

Japan Spring of 1951
Al Meister sent this picture to his future wife Joan Saton, from Japan. "All my love. Al"
In 2006, Al and Joan celebrated their 53rd wedding anniversary.
Picture: Al Meister

His medical unit, located right on the 38th parallel, was short doctors. "Because of that I got stuck with doing things that normally you (*enlisted*) wouldn't be allowed to do." Al was an enlisted Sergeant, but he says he was, "accepted as a semi-official member of the 38th parallel medical society. The only non-commissioned member."

No-one wore uniforms, rank or insignia, when they were treating the wounded.

"During one attack, when we had a lot of casualties, I had ordered whole blood. They sent a Captain up from 8th Army with a whole lot of artificial plasma. He was going to use that. I wouldn't let him." A Sergeant giving orders to a Captain? The Captain was a little miffed when he found out, but Al had the support of his commander. The Captain wasn't miffed enough to take on the Division Surgeon. It all worked out.

Al downplays the two "Bronze Stars" he was awarded in Korea. "That was just given out." For the record "Bronze Stars" are awarded for outstanding achievement in a combat zone. They are not "just given out." Al wouldn't say anything more about it.

He turned down a battlefield commission because he would have had to extend his time in the Army for six months. The pay of a 2nd Lieutenant was less than he was being paid already, anyway.

No reservation in his opinion of being a corpsman and his medical fraternity, "If you look at the awards for heroism given in Iraq, check out how many of them were hospital corpsmen or medical personnel. Over half of them," he says.

I asked him about the inevitable comparison with the movie and television series "MASH." He laughed right out loud. "Well." He laughed again. "There's some truth and a lot of Hollywood in that series. I used to watch it. I enjoyed watching it. It was a long way from the truth."

Al went back to nursing after he got out, long enough to finish his college and a Masters Degree from the University of Maine. He became a "Fishery Scientist" after that, for the rest of his working life. He headed up the "Atlantic Salmon Program."

What have you done since you retired, I asked? "Nothing; a little hunting, a little fishing...not much." He did do some consulting for a short time, until his wife retired.

What's your outstanding memory of your time in the military? "Getting out!"

Al Meister, Bangor, Fall of 2005
His hat is from the KWVA. (Korean War Veterans
Association) His "Bronze Star" is the top medal.
Photo: Al Meister

It's a big operation with around sixty-five full time employees; double that during the busy tree and wreath season in the fall. Doug approaches each day with just about the same enthusiasm and energy that he had to start the company back in 1955, soon after his tour with the air force. He had summer jobs but needed some winter cash, so he scratched together enough money to buy a tractor-trailer truck. He drove it to Milbridge from his home in New Jersey. He stayed at the Atlantic House that night. The next morning he picked up a load of Christmas trees, took them back and sold them. The rest, as the saying goes, "is history."

Doug has a bit of that too; history that is. He's 76 years old and still puts in about twelve hours every single day. He agrees, "He's been lucky. "It's not my fault that I've got good genes. I've had good fortune."

In all reality, his time in the U.S.Air Force is probably the more quiet part of his life, although he did drive racecars. He wasn't suppose to. A crash during a race nearly got him in trouble. He hobbled to work with his injuries. The Air Force never found out about the crash. Doug retired from racing, until he returned to civilian life.

Wall Township, NJ, 1950
Doug Kell with the checkered flag at the end of a race in Wall Stadium.
Photo: Doug Kell

"I lived for racing for a number of years." Doug says. He drove at Darlington; the only super speedway at the time. He drove at Daytona, when part of that track still went along the beach. It was well before the extraordinarily popular "NASCAR" came on the scene. He did pretty well, but racing was expensive. "There wasn't enough money for anybody to get along as a driver so there was a lot of bootlegging."

A sly smile spread across his face, when I asked him if he had ever delivered a load of bootleg liquor. "When you were one of the group you couldn't stay away from it," he says. The bootlegging and the loss of a close friend in a crash, was enough, and so he walked away from it. "It just wasn't for me."

The Korean War caused Doug two-year career in military service. He was activated from the National Guard in New Jersey.

Doug ended up with the wing inspector's office in Japan. He worked on the logistics of transferring a whole bomb-wing across the Pacific for the first time, refueling the planes over Hawaii. He says his experience in the military was short but beneficial. He's glad he did it.

Mid-Air Refueling 1923
Capt. Lowell Smith and Lt. John Richter, used a simple hose to accomplish the first air-to-air refueling of planes.
Photo: National Archives

A civilian again, his life accelerated. He rode around the country, painting church steeples and water tanks, for a while. He worked as a deep-sea diver, and a boating guide in the Bahamas, and became a licensed pilot "I've tried every way I know to kill myself."

Looking back, he says, "I've had lots of failures, but I've had more successes than I've had failures......and I have the courage to have another failure tomorrow....because I'll never have another success, if I'm not willing to risk failure.

The Army recruiter was next. There, they could enlist at eighteen with their parent's permission. Begrudgingly her parents signed, and on the tenth of November 1949, Delores left Bangor for Woman's Army Corp Basic Training. "For me to make that choice to join the service was the very first choice I made for myself in my whole life." She became a medic.

She went through basic at Camp Lee in Virginia and spent the next two years in San Antonio, Fort Sam Houston and the Brook Army Medical Center. She was beginning to think there wasn't time for her to be sent overseas. "Wrong!" She spent the last year of her enlistment at a hospital on Okinawa.

Delores praised her leaders at several points during our conversation. She says they, and a couple of events broadened her education of life. .

One event happened when her softball team went to town and stopped at a neighborhood bar. One of her team members was African-American. Delores remembers the bartender's reaction. "He said is she colored?' I said, God she's black as a stove. How black you gotta be before you're black? He said, 'I can't wait on her." Delores had never seen segregation before. "I was insulted. I didn't think of her as black. She was my friend!"

Another encounter at the Brook Army Medical Center has stayed with her too. A soldier had been brought back to "BAMC" from the freezing winter in Korea. "For several weeks we had coffee breaks together." She took him to coffee, in his wheelchair, for about a month. The last time she saw him, he didn't have an afghan over his legs. "I saw two feet amputated at the ankles (from frost bite). Being a person who loved to dance, I realized the sacrifice he had made for me. She said she felt helpless that she couldn't do more. Delores says she never got the soldiers name and has wondered about him for the rest of her life. "I still pray for him every day," she says.

Delores came home to raise five children. She had six. One died shortly after birth. One of her sons, Mark, is a Cardiac Doctor and a Major Serving in the Army. He recently completed a tour of duty in Iraq.

July 2005: Delores and her son Major Mark Hainer. Mark had just returned from Iraq. Photo: Courtesy Delores Hainer

On Veterans Day 2005, Mark sent his mother a card. The front reads: *"Many years have passed since the Korean War, but the freedom you fought to preserve has been a lasting gift, one still treasured today."*

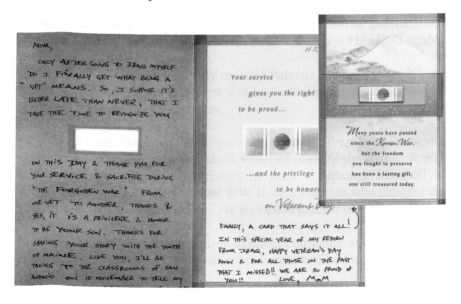

In his message to his mother, Mark says, *"Mom, Only after going to Iraq myself do I finally get what being a "Vet" means. So, I suppose it's better late than never, that I take the time to recognize you on this day & thank you for your service & sacrifice during "The Forgotten War." From one vet to another, thanks & yes, it is a privilege & honor to be your son. Love MmM."* (Mark, Marshall and Marlene Hainer; Mark, his son and wife.)

Del's coaching career ended in 1978 when he was selected to be the fourth President of Husson College, where he had graduated thirty years earlier.

The college was floundering and in danger of closing. Del says during his first month, "I wrote a letter to every one of our creditors and I said it may take some time but I guarantee that every bill that Husson owes will be paid." The response was positive....the bills were paid, and the downward course was turned around. Today, Husson is a vibrant growing institution. It was very close!

In 1985, two years before his retirement, Husson presented Delmont Merrill with an Honorary Doctor of Business Administration Degree.

As you can see, Del Merrill has done a lot in his lifetime. I asked him if he could pick a high point? Without hesitation, "When I married my wife, "Betty Ann." They had been married fifty-seven years when Betty Ann lost a very long battle with cancer in January of 2007.

Today Dr. Merrill is president of the family business in Ellsworth.

WILLIAM "BILL" KNIGHT

Bangor, Maine

U.S.Army..............May 27, 1940 – August 31, 1945
U.S, Navy..............July 1957 – July 1981

Chief, Engineerman

"Very seldom a day that I'm not out there."

Bill Knight is a "Troop Greeter." Oh, he's a veteran....Army-Air Force during WW II. He spent another twenty-one years in the Navy later on, too. We'll talk about that too, but first, Bill Knight "Troop Greeter."

Bangor's location on the northeastern coast, and the long runway, left behind when the Air Force cleared out in 1968, make it a logical refueling point for troop planes heading to and returning from world trouble spots.

Most of us still swell with pride as we remember the images of the first planes coming back from "Desert Storm" in 1991.

Bangor International Airport, March 7, 1991
A returning soldier proudly flies the American Flag from the top of a plane returning him from Desert Storm.
Photo: Cole Museum, Courtesy Hilda Gott and Wilbur Watson

As the troops entered the hallway, connecting the international and domestic terminals, the troop greeters were already in a receiving line. Since the "Gulf War," every single soldier, sailor, airman, marine or coast guardsman passing through Bangor has been greeted by smiles, cheers, a handshake and most receive a welcoming hugs. Bill says, "It's a wonderful feeling. It makes you glad."

"You can imagine what shape we were in when we finally arrived," Phil wrote.

Philip Clukey prior to his deployment in 1942
Photo: Courtesy Mrs. Dorothy Clukey

After a seasick trip across the Pacific, Phil ended up in New Zealand. The Japanese had just been halted at Guadalcanal in their march through the Solomon Islands. They had retreated to New Georgia to build the Munda Airfield. His unit was ordered to keep that from happening.

Phil says, "It was a major battle with severe loss of life and many casualties, teaching us the realities of jungle warfare." He says, "We were subject to enemy fire, we were continually digging foxholes, some out of dirt and mud but many out of coral, which was like digging in cement. We encountered swamps, rain forests, coconut-log pillboxes, snipers in trees, and moving in endless mud." On two occasions, men sharing a foxhole with Phil were killed by snipers.

Munda Airfield August 1943. Assault forces had to clear away debris to make the airfield usable for U.S. Forces.
This Japanese "Zero" was camouflaged in an improvised coconut and palm shelter.

Photo: U.S. Marines Collection

Phil's group also fought the Japanese into the mountains of New Guinea, and was involved in the capture of Manila in the Philippines.

South Pacific 1943: Philip Clukey during one of the few quiet times.
Photo: Courtesy Mrs. Dorothy Clukey

Phil's son Bruce recalls, "As a boy, asking him if he had killed anyone in the war? He changed the subject."

173

Phil's discharge was delayed for a few days while the army came through with a partial plate for his back teeth. That had been promised to him when he signed up.

He attended the Maine School of Commerce after he got out. We now know that as Husson College. He was a partner, and traveled the state representing Wights Sporting Goods in Bangor.

Looking back at the war, Spam was a staple in the rations provided to GIs during WW II. GIs called Spam "Roosevelt Sausage." Troops in the Pacific also got lots of Australian canned lamb or mutton. Of course there were coconuts growing everywhere.

In the notes Dorothy provided, Phil wrote, "Spam, mutton and coconuts are foods I dislike to this day."

PHILIP T. CLUKEY
June 4, 1919 – August 31, 2006
Photo: Courtesy Mrs. Dorothy Clukey

BURLEIGH V. SHOREY

Milford, Maine

U.S. Navy........................November 1942 – February 1946

GM3, Submariner

"We got news that Japan had ceased hostilities.   Wow! What a day that was.

Burleigh Shorey was a "Plank Owner" on the Pintado – SS/AGSS 387. He was on board the submarine on September 15, 1943, the day the boat was launched by the Portsmouth Navy Yard at Kittery.

September 15, 1943: Portsmouth Navy Yard, Kittery, Maine
The launch of the United States submarine Pintado (SS-387)
Photo: US Navy

Burleigh was an Enfield boy. He quit high school and went to work to help his family out. "It was during the depression....the family was having a hard time. I said I'll go to work in the woods."

The war was on and the military beckoned. Burleigh thought the Marine Corps would be a good fit but his father would have no part of that. He agreed to sign for Burleigh to go into the Navy. Burleigh was just seventeen years old. His dad had to sign for him to get in.

The submarine service happened, sort of by chance. "On the bulletin board, it said anyone who volunteered for the submarine service and gets accepted gets a 15 day leave." Burleigh said, "I'd do anything for that leave."

Portsmouth Navy Yard, Kittery, Maine
The crew of the Pintado. Burleigh Shorey is in the third row on the right, partially obscured by the man in front of him.
Photo: US Navy

Burleigh got accepted. He rode the sub out of Portsmouth, through the Panama Canal and into the war in the Pacific. He nearly got left behind during sea trials off Key West Florida. "We was practicing diving without the diving alarm. The diving officer would holler 'dive, dive!' I didn't hear it. The wind was blowing." Burleigh looked around and noticed everyone else gone, and the boat was blowing the ballast tanks. "I headed for the top of the periscope." The water was coming up around him. "The worst part of it was the sharks that followed the boat."

With the Gulf of Mexico licking at Burleigh's feet, the quartermaster completed his count inside. Three men had gone out and only two had returned. He halted the dive. Burleigh smiled, "Boy that was good!"

After the war, Corwin Mendenhall, the Executive Officer on the Pintado wrote a book about the patrols of the sub, published by Naval Institute Press.* He titled the book "Submarine Diary." This is a brief excerpt from his account of "Pintado's First Patrol."

'16 May, Having completed all preparations for patrol, Pintado was underway after lunch headed for Midway in company with Shark and Pilotfish.'

The submarines patrolled in "wolfpacks" of three boats.

'We were scheduled to reach our patrol area just west of Saipan on 29. May. Allied landings were due to take place there in early June and the objective of the wolfpack was to prevent Jap reinforcements from reaching Saipan before the Allied troops went ashore.'

'17-19 May, En route to Midway we conducted daily drills in wolfpack communications, training dives, tracking drills, fire control and school of the boat. On the nineteenth a battle surface drill was held during which five rounds were fired from the 4-inch gun and one pan of ammunition from each 20-mm gun..'

Pacific Ocean 1944.
The Pintado underway on patrol.
The sub is named for the Pintado, a large mackerel-like fish, found along the Florida coasts and the West Indies.
Photo: US Navy

'20 May, Pintado moored along side Bang in the nest at the side of tender Proteus and topped off with fuel and water.'

May 20, 1944 Midway Lagoon
Sub Tender Proteus with
submarines Bang, Pintado
and Pilotfish.
Photo: US Navy

On the 21st, the three subs were underway again, heading for their patrol area, just west of Saipan Island, but they were slowed along the way and reached the straights of Formosa in the daylight. Burleigh says there was concern, Japanese troops would spot them. "They always kidded me because I was from Maine. A guy came down and said 'do you know what I just saw up there on shore?' I said no.....hard telling what you're going to see. He said, 'we see a guy there with a University of Maine sweatshirt on.' Just trying to tease me because I'm from Maine." The sub made it through undetected.

Back to the diary:

'On 22 May, we moved the calendar ahead to 23 May as we crossed the International Date Line.'

'29 May, at 0500 the subs submerged for the day only thirty-seven miles from the patrol area.'

Burleigh says their mission was, "Find um and Sink um."

It was about midday on June 4th the Pintado spotted smoke from a Japanese convoy headed toward Saipan. The Shark sank two of the ships. Pintado made her first kills shortly before noon on June 6. (D-Day in Normandy) A spread of torpedos hit the 5,652 ton Havre Maru and the 2,825 ton Kashimasan Maru. The explosion tore the ships apart. The bow and the stern of the Havre Maru were both pointing up in the air as she sank.

The Pintado sank thirteen ships in all during her patrols and damaged an air craft carrier. Burleigh says, "That felt pretty good."

They took their share of abuse too. One time they were hundreds of feet under the surface, dodging depth charges, for seventy hours. The sub had just air enough to stay down seventy-two hours.

Burleigh's account of that time: "We couldn't shake um. They'd ping us and you'd hear the sound right through the ship, and then you'd know what's going to happen next. You'd hear the detonator click and then came the charge." Enemy ships dropped eighty depth charges on the Pintado that time. Burleigh says the explosions broke air lines...paint chips and pieces of insulation flew around, but they escaped. They were lucky. Fifty two U.S. subs were lost during the war. The Pintado got away when they sent "Alka Seltzer" out through a torpedo tube in a signaling device. The enemy ships chased the "Alka Seltzer." Burleigh says "It sounded like propellers, woosh, woosh." The enemy pinged the decoy sound and the sub sneaked away.

Burleigh Shorey, Bangor, Maine – November 2006:
What was the best thing about your military career? "When I got discharged."
Photo: Don Colson

Some Navy officials credited the Pinato wolfpack with eliminating one full Japanese Division from the fighting on Saipan.

The Pintado received the "Presidential Unit Citation for their successful patrols. It reads in part: ***The Pintado achieved a record of heroism in combat in keeping with the highest traditions of the United States Naval Service.*** The citation is signed by James Forrestal, Secretary of the Navy.

The Pinato was off Tokyo Bay when the war ended. Burleigh remembers it well. "We got news that Japan had ceased hostilities. Wow! What a day that was. The medical personnel had brandy for wounds, and we all had a good sip of brandy."

Burleigh and Laura Shorey celebrated their sixtieth anniversary on October 20, 2006.

*"Submarine Diary, The Silent Stalking of Japan"   Author: Corwin Mendenhall. Published by, U.S. Naval Institute, March 7, 1995

CHARLES TITCOMB

Bangor, Maine

U.S. Army-Air Force.........November, 1942 – January 25, 1946

Sergeant, Teletype Operator

"They hit eight of our planes. They killed forty-eight men."

Charlie Titcomb spends a lot his time today volunteering. "I just like people," he says. It shows. Charlie is an outgoing guy...almost always with a smile on his face.

He grew up in Newport. He came to Bangor to attend the Maine School of Commerce. (*Today Husson College*) That determined the direction he would go in the Air Corps. One of the interviewers, in Miami, where Charlie went to basic training, asked, "I see you've been to business college?" "Yes I have." "I presume you can type?" "Yes I can." Charlie says, "The next thing I knew there was a group of us on a troop train. I didn't know where I was going." He found out; when the train stopped in Omaha, Nebraska, where he was marched off to teletype school.

After school his class was shipped to Washington, D.C. The group was split up, with nine sent to Presque Isle, Maine. That was Charlie's first choice, but he stayed in Washington at the Pentagon. New York guys went to Presque Isle. The Maine guy goes to Washington, DC. How often have we heard about that kind of thing happening?

Charlie spent a year and a half, at the Pentagon, under General "Hap" Arnold. General Henry Harley "Hap" Arnold was an Air Force pioneer. The Wright brothers taught him to fly. He soloed on May 13, 1911. He was commander of the US Army

Gen. H.H. "Hap" Arnold. His aunt gave him the name of "Hap" for happy. Photo: USAF

Air Forces from 1941 until 1945, and the only person to be a five-star general in two armed services. Charlie says he didn't have any contact with the General ....."saw him a couple of times."

WORLD WAR I

Bangor, Maine, June 22, 1916
The soldiers of Company "G" march down Exchange
Street to the train station; bedrolls holding all their gear
on one shoulder...their rifle over the other.
Photo: Courtesy Francis Allen

WILLIAM HUTCHINSON

Stonington, Maine

U.S. Marines........March 1943 – July 1946

Corporal, Bomb Disposal

"They put it on us in good shape."

Bill Hutchinson is made out of the same stuff as most Maine fishermen....solid, honest, reliable....usually low-key. Bill was fishing with his brother when WW II broke out. They had a hundred or so lobster traps in the water. Times were not quite as bad for the people on Stonington, as they were at lots of other places. There was work in the quarry, and at the sardine factory. Quite a few Stonington men made money lobstering.....many others worked on yachts. Bill was pretty comfortable when the "draft" notice came. He went willingly though.... "Happy" to serve his country.

Maui 1944
William Hutchingon, a young U.S. Marine. Most of the Marines who invaded Iwo Jima, trained in the Hawaiian Islands. Photo: Courtesy Bill Hutchinson

Bill's another of our guys who ended up in the "Hell on Earth" that was Iwo Jima, in February of 1945. He went ashore on February 20th.....day two of the invasion. "They tried to get us in and the ship got hit a couple of times." Finally, "We hit the beach....the sand was up to here." He touched his knee with his hand. "We had, of course, packs on our backs....rifles.....it was quite a struggle."

The unrelenting bombardment from the dug in Japanese continued. "They put it to us in good shape. We kept hearing these shells going over all night....going whoosh and then bang. We said, them's ours, but it was the 'Japs." It was pretty close that night, he says. He dug a foxhole, but his unit moved up before he could crawl in. The foxhole took a direct hit.

Bill was part of a bomb disposal team, assigned to the 5th Amphibious Corps, attached to the 4th Marine Division. "We took up mines.....and bombs....we took the fuses out....and the big sixteen inch projectiles, duds that didn't explode, we had to take the fuses out."

Iwo Jima, February 1945
Bill Hutchinson's bomb disposal team. Bill is second from the right.
Photo: Courtesy Bill Hutchinson

American planes and ships bombarded the island all during 1944. That's why the Japanese gave up on their airfields, and dug the elaborate maze of tunnels, to hide their 22,000 troops. Bill says U.S. observers flew over the island and didn't see a thing. "There was one man in one of the pictures," he said.

The Japanese had dug in parts of wrecked planes on the beach, as shields and barriers. They also buried bombs in the sand and placed mines right over them. Bill and the other bomb disposal guys dug into the sand with wire probes to locate the bombs and mines.

"They had these tunnels, my gosh, all over the island." As U.S. forces gained control of the island, Bill's unit had to make sure things were secure. "We went all around checking those caves to see if there was anybody in there, and to remove unexploded mines and bombs."

He saw the flag at the top of Suriabachi too. "I noticed it that morning. It was like looking over Green Head here. I knew that they (*U.S. troops*) had got to the top." According to reports after the war, U.S troops found a unit of Japanese observers, as many as a hundred, who had dug in near the top of the mountain, had committed suicide.

He spent thirty-one days under fire on the island. He remembers the times the Japanese would wheel their big guns out of the caves and bombard them. "We'd lay right down flat...crawl underneath a shovel if we could." Lots of guys got hit. "Them little Jeeps was coming down this trail there all the time, one right behind the other, with double stretchers on um." Somehow, Bill's unit didn't lose a single man.

Bill returned to Maui on April 12, 1945 the day President Franklin Roosevelt died. He didn't have enough points to go home, after the Japanese surrendered, so he became part of the occupation force....to help set up a new government, and get things back together in Japan, after the war. "We had to disarm everything." He says it was a good experience. "There was no animosity at all."

Bill went back to lobstering when he returned. He fished until he retired in 2001. A bunch of those years he fished all year long, even when the lobsters moved off shore into deep water in the winter. Many days it would take two or three hours to reach his traps. Many of those days it was well below zero.

Yep, solid, honest and tough too.......tougher than most....Bill Hutchinson is a Maine lobsterman, who for a little more than three years of his life, did his country proud too.

overcast. Boat is pitching slightly. Spotted a boat. It was friendly because it didn't fire. There are about 13,000 men and 1,000 women on board."

The trip went pretty well through the weekend. On Saturday they had to begin wearing their steel helmets. Enemy planes became a greater threat, as they got farther out in the Atlantic.

Sunday night/Monday morning, the weather changed...the ocean became angry.

"Mon. Feb 7, 1944. Last night was rough. I don't think anyone slept more than ten mins. all night. Mess kits, boxes, and everything loose, was falling all over the place. I went down to chow this morning and the place is a wreck. Tables and seats smashed...fellows cut from nails...clothes covered with food."

He sighted land and lots of other ships on Tuesday.

"Tues. Feb 8, 1944. I think the land is Scotland. Dropped anchor at about 6 PM, in port not far from Glascow, Scotland. Pretty country."

After bouncing from camp to camp for a few days, Harry was assigned to the 9th Air Force Headquarters, as a wireless operator, at Uxbridge. "I saw my first "Buzz Bomb" flying over us. It missed and landed a block away, blowing up a whole block of brick houses."

London 1945.
Left, A (V-1) "buzz bomb cuts its' motor, and dives into the Piccadilly section of London.
Photo: National Archives
Below; **Duxford Air Base, outside London.**
Harry took this picture of a "Buzz Bomb" on display, in 2006.

The Vergeltungswaffe-1 (V-1). GIs called them "buzz bombs' because the primitive jet-like motors made a buzzing sound, until the motor shut off, just before the rocket would hit.

That's when people worried...the silence. The Germans launched the missile-like bombs, from "ski jump" launch sites, along the French coast.

Harry got into London for two or three days, while he was stationed in Uxbridge. "Black outs, at night, were kind of exciting. Vehicles traveled with small slits in their headlights. All windows and doorways had hanging drapes over them, so you only saw shadows of people."

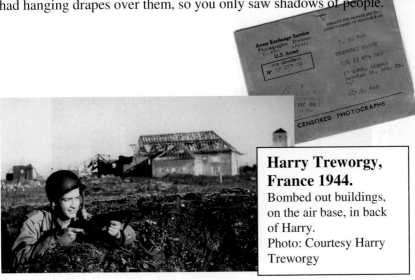

Harry Treworgy, France 1944.
Bombed out buildings, on the air base, in back of Harry.
Photo: Courtesy Harry Treworgy

His unit was involved in D-Day activities too. (June 6, 1944). They sent deception messages to phony ships, to throw the Germans off. "We didn't know what we were sending or receiving; only letter groups in code."

He was in France when the German's launched their Ardennes offensive. *(Battle of the Bulge)* "I stood guard duty at our base many nights during heavy fog. What to do? I had my carbine and was all alone. Should I ask questions about America first, or shoot first and ask questions later?" Fortunately, he didn't have to do either. "It was the only time I really felt scared."

On November 26, 1945 Harry was on the USS Madawaska, a "Victory" ship, as it left La Havre, France for the United States. He was discharged from military service on December 10, 1945.

Harry went back and got his degree from the University of Maine.

scarce.....money was scarce. He went to the University of Maine the year after he graduated from Brewer High, and then transferred down to the Maine Maritime Academy in Castine. Graduation day for his class was July 1st, 1942. Frank was sworn into the Navy, the same day. "I got my orders. I left for west coast and picked up my first ship," the USS Bellatrix, (AKA-3) an attack cargo ship.

USS Bellatrix (AKA-3)
(top)
underway in the mid 1950s. She was reactivated during the Korean War...transferred to Peru in 1963. In 1991 she was sold for scrap.
Photo: Naval Historical center.

The engineering crew on the Bellatrix. (Bottom)
Frank Jewell is on the far right.
Photo: Courtesy Frank Jewell

Frank was off shore, on June, 15, 1944, on the Bellatrix, as the 2nd and 4th Marine Divisions and the 27th Infantry Division, landed on Saipan. "We put our boats over and took our cargo ashore," and soldiers from the 27th Infantry. "I guess we were unloaded in a couple of days."

By mid-1944, Allied troops had captured the Solomon Islands, the Gilbert Islands and New Guinea. Saipan and the other islands in the Marianas, the Caroline Islands and Palau Island remained as the main Japanese line of defense. By July 7, with no place to hide or run, Imperial Japanese Army commander Lt. Gen, Yoshitsugu Saito ordered his remaining men ahead in a suicidal banzai charge, and then killed himself. The Allies took control of Saipan.

Frank says, "We didn't have too much trouble with the air war. The Japanese were pretty well grounded out then. There was a lot going on, getting the troops ashore. Our battle ships were bombarding the island. They were standing about 15 miles off the coast. It was busy, and I suppose you'd say a little scary."

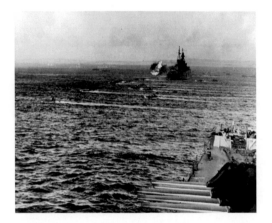

Saipan June 15, 1944 The USS Birmingham is in the foreground; the cruiser firing, in the distance is the Indianapolis. Photo: US Navy

The Bellatrix was sent back to the states for repairs after Saipan.

In December of 1945, Frank was transferred to the USS Bronx, a Navy Attack Transport. They made trips to Shanghai, and the Philippines. It was much more pleasant duty, with the war over.

Frank remembers a lot of happy troops, "We made trips across the Pacific on what they called "Magic Carpet Duty," bringing hundreds of happy troops back to the states."

While Frank was crossing the Pacific, Barbara was seeing to it that sailors out there got their mail. Ask any veteran to list the most important things during the war, and I'll bet at least eight out of ten will say receiving mail....maybe even ten out of ten. Word from home was awfully important.

Barbara's father was in the Navy in WW I; she had two brothers in the Navy in 1944, so it seemed like the right thing to do. "I taught school in Eddington but during the year, I saw signs "Join the Waves" and help the men, and that sort of inspired me."

US Navy "Waves" recruiting poster (1944)...one of many done by artist John Philip Falter. Photo: Naval Historical Center

She ended up at the Fleet Post Office, in New York City, first. "The Navy took the "Manhattan Tower" hotel at 76th and Broadway." That was her barracks. "I felt I was doing a good thing, getting that mail off to those boys."

Barbara Jewell,
June 1945
After her transfer to the records office in San Francisco.
Photo: Courtesy Barbara Jewell

Barbara "Law" Jewell went back to teaching after she got out. Frank spent thirty-five years in the insurance business. He stayed in the Navy reserve in Bangor, until he got his twenty years for retirement.

Oh yes, after Frank couldn't find that "other girl" in New York, Barbara says, "We got together." Then the Navy helped. "I was transferred out to California." She was re-assigned to the fleet post office in San Francisco. "He was stationed at San Diego. His ship came up to San Francisco, and we went from there." They still are, sixty-one years later.

Barbara & Frank Jewell
Veterans Day 2004, in Bangor.
Photo: Courtesy the Jewells

LOUIS P. PARE

Brewer, Maine

U.S. Marines........................August 7, 1943 – February 15, 1946
U.S. Army...............................March 1947 – November 1949

Corporal, Infantry-Service Battalion

"The smell of death was over the whole area."

World War II never ended for Louis Pare.

Louis turned seventeen on July 11, 1943. Three weeks later he was at the Marine recruiter's office. On August 7, 1943 he was sworn in to the United States Marines Corps, 5th Service Battalion, 5th Marine division. Eighteen months later, eighteen years old, he waded ashore under heavy fire, on Iwo Jima.

Louis Pare,
During his tour of duty with the US Marines.
Photo: Courtesy Louis Pare

197

New Britain is "Mud" in Bill's South Pacific trio of misery..."Crud, Mud, and Blood." Guadalcanal was "Crud." "I was dirty all the time." He says. The Marines had New Britain pretty much under control by the time he got there. He remembers most, the unrelenting rain. "It was mud, mud, mud.....rain, rain, rain." He says, "New Britain was a horrible place. If they were ever going to give the world an enema, that's where they'd put the tube, at least in the rainy season."

He was wounded on "Bloody" Peleliu, one of the most costly battles in the entire war in the South Pacific. Another Marine with Maine connections, Major Everett Pope received the "Medal of Honor" fighting on Peleliu.

Bill was in another section of the island when he was injured, "Our platoon was just moving up that day when we started to get hit by mortar or artillery fire." He was trying to escape the war for a couple of minutes when a shell hit. He still doesn't know if it was a mortar or artillery shell. I never saw it. I was in a shell hole smoking a cigarette....taking life easy." Someone yelled for a medic. "I crawled up to the top of the shell hole to see what was happening.. Just about then, bang!" Doctors on a hospital ship and then a hospital on Manus Island fixed him up. He didn't know at the time, but that was the last combat he would see.

During the year that followed, once his wounds healed, he did guard duty at the Naval Air Station in Brunswick and Auburn for a while. He was at Camp Pendleton in California preparing to go overseas again.....preparing for the attack on the Japanese mainland, when the war ended.

"You were scared.... course you were scared, but you knew you had to be there." He chuckled. "There wasn't much you could do about it."

Louise and Bill Park,
October 2006
They were married on October 1, 1947
Photo: Courtesy the Parks

ROBERT GLIDDEN

Orrington, Maine

U.S. Army............................February 1942 – December 1945

Corporal/Technitian, Anti-Aircraft

"I think any young man should have to do it."

Bob Glidden was as enterprising in earlier life, in the military, as he was later on, when he ran his own successful business.

His early time in the military was pretty much like all the others.....basic training.....special training. Bob learned all about the 90 MM Anti-Aircraft gun. He was with the 738th Anti-Aircraft Artillery.

The 90 MM cannon had a range of just under 18 miles. It could hit a plane 10 miles in the air. The range was limited by its 30 second fuse.

Photo: Aurelio Hecket

He became company bugler. "I didn't have to go on patrol or nothing....or any guard duty. I always had to be on call for assembly or taps...........and all those things."

Blowing the bugle was just one part of his diverse military career. He was also assistant manager of the Post Exchange, assistant manager of a supply yard, and he did a little business of his own on the side.

Every afternoon he was a barber, and at night he did some sewing for the guys. "I used to take suntan pants and cut um off and make shorts."

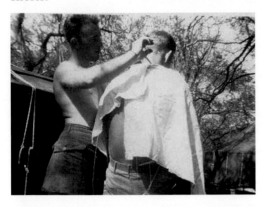

Saipan 1944.

Bob Glidden received twenty-five cents for his haircuts.

Photo: Courtesy Robert Glidden

He got twenty-five cents a piece for his haircuts.......doesn't remember how much they paid him for his sewing. "Wasn't much."

Sooner or later he knew he'd find the war.... but even that was delayed.

After nine months of training on Hawaii, Bob was on a victory ship, going through the Marshall Islands, part of Task Force 78 heading for Saipan. "I don't think the captain wanted to go to Saipan very bad."

They were navigating a narrow channel, when the guy on watch reported seeing water breaking over shallow coral. Bob says the captain replied, "You watch the breakers. I'll keep the ship." It was about that time the ship went right up onto the shore. It was so high; the propellers were out of water. All attempts to pull it off the beach failed. Bob says, "We stayed on that island for thirty days and just drank beer and played baseball."

He did make it to Saipan eventually, and on a 90 MM gun, as the Japanese patrols came over. "Every night they'd start coming in and we'd have these raids for two or three hours. The biggest thing that scart me was they dropped a "photo bomb," *(a very large, very bright flare)* to take a picture of our area. He had never seen or heard of a "photo bomb" before. "It lit up like the sun come up, you know. Oh God, it was bright."

He went back to work for Bangor Auto Body when he got out......stayed there for twenty-four years, then he opened his own auto body shop, and ran it for fourteen years, before he retired.

Looking back, Bob says, "Frankly it was a good experience, and I think any young man should have to do it."

Bob Glidden visited the WW II Memorial in Washington, D.C. in September of 2005.

Photo: Courtesy Robert Glidden

WORLD WAR II MEMORIAL

World War II Memorial, Washington, D.C
The national WW II Memorial commemorates the
sacrifices and celebrates the victories of the WW II
generation.
It was dedicated on May 29, 2004

PAUL MARSHALL WILBUR

Hermon, Maine

U.S. Marines..............February 12, 1942 – February 11, 1946

Corporal, Infantry

"You crawled down into the sand, scared to death."

"I was quite a patriotic young man....always have been. My father was a vet of WW I, and when the war broke out with Japan, I told my father I feel like I should go and do what I can."

Paul Wilbur was still in high school on December 7, 1941 when the Japanese bombed Pearl Harbor, but he wanted to get into the war and do his part. He wasn't unlike most young men then. Most waited to finish school before they signed up. Paul didn't. He turned seventeen in January of 1942. His dad signed for him, and on February 12, 1942 he was off to the Marines. For Paul, high school would wait.

Bangor, Maine 1942
Paul Wilber at home on leave, before shipping out to the
South Pacific.
Photo: Courtesy Paul Wilber

It didn't take long for him to find the war. A few weeks of basic training and he was on a train bound for California and ultimately the island of New Caledonia in the Coral Sea. Allied forces had just turned back the Japanese invasion of Port Moreby, New Guinea. The "Battle of Coral Sea" is said to be one of the early turning points of the War in the Pacific. It was the first time aircraft carriers squared off, and the first naval battle in history in which ships from neither side sighted each other, nor fired directly on each other. Although the US lost the heavy carrier USS Lexington, Japanese forces were so damaged they were weakened for the "Battle of Midway" a month later.

The Japanese hadn't reached New Caledonia yet and the US was building forces there to keep them away. Paul's job was to string communication lines and, he says, "I was generating hydrogen gas for barrage balloons." The balloons were raised on long steel cables as a defense against enemy bombers. "Paul says the balloons...they'd go up there, *(5000 feet or more)* way above the clouds and these planes would come in for a bomb run, and they wouldn't see the cables. The cables would clip the wing right off um. It'd do quite a job on um really."

From there, the Marines moved Paul to Guadalcanal. The war there had been raging for several weeks by the time he got there. The "Battle of Guadalcanal" was fought between August 7, 1942 and February 9, 1943. Historians say it was a decisive campaign of the war. Once again, Paul's job was drive truck and set up communications. He had a close call. "An artillery shell came right through the roof of my truck. The damn thing didn't go off. It scared the hell out of me. Other than that, I was alright."

Things were going to get even hotter for him. Late October, Paul's 3rd Marine Division was poised off Bougainville. US Navy ships had been

210

bombarding it for seventy-two hours, nonstop. US planes bombed the island softening it up for the landing. November 1, 1943 the command came, 'Over the side.' Paul remembers it well. "We started climbing down over the side of these troop carriers....with our rifles, back packs and everything you needed to fight a war with."

"We went in and no more had we started ashore than the Japanese started throwing artillery shells at us." Boats, on both sides of Paul's, took direct hits. "The minute we hit the beach, Japanese planes came in and started strafing the beach. You had no place to go! You crawled down into the sand, scared to death." He crawled for cover in the Jungle.

The battle to control Bougainville went on for twelve days, before US Troops took control. Paul says, "Japanese were dug in. They were dug in something fierce. All that bombing......all that shelling, never bothered um a bit."

Once again Paul lived in fox holes, drove trucks and helped establish communication and radar links. He says he saw lots of fire but never saw a Japanese solder. "I never killed one," he says.

Bougainville 1944
At night the Japanese would infiltrate US lines.
During the day US GIs found them and killed them.
Photo: National Archives

He spent only a few weeks in boot camp ....physicals, shots, new uniforms, calisthenics and marching practice....."We were the worst marchers in the boot camp, He says. "To this day I haven't seen a sailor who could march."

And then he was off to U.S. Navy Mine Warfare School at Yorktown, Virginia. Like boot camp, school was accelerated too. The war was on and minesweepers were needed. Most of the old sweepers were sunk or scrapped after War I, and sweepers were needed in the battle zones.

Fran was part of a new crew preparing for a ship that was still being built. They learned fast.... two days a week in classrooms, and the rest of the week on a training sweeper, clearing miles German submarines had planted in the mouth of Chesapeake Bay.

On September 24th, 1942 Fran boarded his first ship at Orange, Texas: A brand new wooden hulled minesweeper.... "YMS 71." Shake down cruises and an incident with acid in the main engines slowed them down, and diverted them from an assignment in North Africa. "The bad guys were caught and carted away." He says he never found out what was behind the sabotage.

Sabin River. Texas
The "YMS 71" as it left the yard where it was built.
Photo Fran Zelz

On February 4th, 1943, with their engines repaired, the "YMS 71" headed for the Panama Canal, with Brisbane, Australia and World War II in the Pacific ahead of them. "The trip across, with stops in Bora Bora, Pago Pago, Suva and Novmea was like vacation cruise," He says, "Almost."

They swept....cleared mines inside the barrier reef and worked their way north. The ship got shot up and had to return for repairs several times. Fran says, "Sure I was scared, several times, but not for long. The name of the game was do our job. I really didn't have time to be scared."

He remembers the week they were near New Britain, a Japanese fighter, a "zero" would fly over to see what was going on. "Every afternoon at about two o'clock. We would go to general quarters." The plane would stay up pretty high and leave without any trouble. "He never bothered us," Fran says. "That went on for a week or more. We got used to it."

Then one day the plane came in a lot lower. "He was about fifty feet off the water." Fran, still in his teens, was a gun captain, in charge of the three-inch, fifty-caliber gun on the bow. He told his crew to stand by. "Hold your fire!" The captain commanded from the bridge. The zero made a run at the ship, and as he neared the ship he made a big climbing turn and went away. He made another run. "Don't fire!" the captain commanded. Fran says the zero was very threatening. "I thought the old man had lost his papers or something." "Hold your fire!" The zero broke off again.

Fran says his gun crew was becoming increasingly agitated......urging him to let them fire. They were in a pretty vulnerable place. They had only the gun to get behind and that didn't provide much protection. Deforest Parker, a full blooded Seneca Indian from New York was first loader. "Come on, give me the word," he said as he cradled a three inch round in his arms. "Stand by." Fran told him. "Don't fire!" The captain ordered again.

The zero headed for the ship again, but this time directly at the bow. "The Captain was screaming like a mad-man." But Zelz says this was a different run, and without hesitation, he nodded to Parker. The shell was loaded, and the pointer fired the gun. "The plane was right on top of us.......the thing just blew.....and that was it."

Fran Zelz during a quieter moment at Milne Bay. Photo Fran Zelz

Fran says there were lots of accusations, threats of court martial and prison over the next twenty-four hours, but the next morning, the Captain came to him, apologized and shook his hand. They put the whole incident behind them. Fran got some paint and painted a small Japanese flag on the bridge. The crew of- the "YMS 71" had their first kill. He says he never knew what the captain was thinking.

The ship continued its' mission. It got shot up, and repaired. They lost their engines during a typhoon, but managed to limp into the Philippines for repairs. They took ten Japanese prisoners after a lop-sided gun battle with a small landing craft, near Dutch New Guinea.

The "YMS 71 was part of the (Seventh Fleet).....one of about seven hundred ships in the task force involved in the Leyte Gulf landings. Historians record that as the world's greatest sea battle ever. "It did get noisy, to say the least," Fran says. "We were happy when it was over." The sweeps were often among the first ships in, to clear mines from harbors, for landings.

The courageous career of the "YMS 71" ended one day off the northern shore of Borneo. It was a routine day for them. They were sweeping mines again, but they missed one and hit it. The blast shattered the forward third of the 132 foot long ship.

Near Borneo:
This picture of the "YMS 71" was taken by a sailor on an accompanying "sweep" as munitions on the ship exploded, minutes before it went down. Photo: Fran Zelz

Sympathetic blasts of munitions finished the job. A pocket of air in the stern kept the ship up long enough for Fran to run from depth charge to depth charge, locking them safe. The charges were armed and set at specific depths and would have exploded under survivors and rescue ships as the "YMS 71" sunk if he hadn't.

Seaman Sever, (*Fran doesn't remember his first name*) the lookout on the bow of the boat, was thrown through the air by the blast. Witnesses say they saw arms and legs flying. The man was picked from the water unharmed. Fran says he remembers Sever was a bit angry that his watch had stopped. In all, twenty-six of the twenty-eight crewmembers on the "YMS 71" survived.

That ended the war in the Pacific for Francis Zelz. He was sent back to the states for "Advanced Gunnery" school, in Maryland near Washington, D.C. A visit to a U.S.O. gained him a Christmas season dinner at the home of band leader Harry James. He met President Franklin Roosevelt and movie star Ester Williams.

Fran was on board the, Bath, Maine built U.S.S. Goodrich, DD831 in Casco Bay the day the Japanese surrendered.

The GI bill helped him become an architect.

Bangor, September 2006
Fran Zelz examines his memory wall at his Bangor home.
Photo: Don Colson

WORLD WAR II

Dow Air Force Base, Bangor, Maine
Pvt. John Laslow of Anson was a radioman with the Army
Air Corps. stationed at Dow Field when this picture was
taken in 1943-44,
Photo: Courtesy, Cole Museum – Sheila Laslow

RAYMOND LEE PERKINS, JR.

Orrington, Maine

U.S. Army...........March 12, 1940 – November 9, 1943

Corporal, Artillery/Machine Gunner

"I gave um all I could."

On November 15th, 2006, Ray Perkins sat for his 1,032[nd] interview by a Maine school student. He's been a volunteer part of the "Veteran Interview Program" at the Cole Land Transportation Museum since it began. More than thirteen thousand Maine school students have interviewed a vet in the program, and learned about our great wars. They've heard about important chapters in the history of our country, from eyewitnesses.....from people who were there. They've heard how great our country is, and they have learned first hand that freedom is not free, but precious and worth fighting for, from the people who did.

Bangor, "Veteran Interview Program"
Each year, in the spring and fall at the Cole Land Transportation Museum, students learn about history from the people who were there.
Photo: Cole Land Transportation Museum

Ray fought for our freedom in the South Pacific during WW II. He gave up farming tools for a machine gun. I don't know if he quite planned it that way, but his dislike of working on the Orrington farm, where he grew up, actually got him there. "I'll tell you getting up early in the morning...water the cattle.....weed the garden in the summer, tread hay; as a kid you're thinking, boy I'm being abused." Today he sees it a little differently. "It was a good life. I was lucky."

In 1940 the National Guard offered a break from farming.....a few days away at drills, a longer trip to basic training in Florida. Ray signed on with the 152nd Field Artillery of the Maine Army National Guard. That summer he got his training at the armory in Brewer. In the fall, his unit moved to New York for field training. That's when the picture began to clear.

Ray had been in New York for just a few days, when President Franklin Delano Roosevelt came by their camp, and told them he was federalizing all New England Guard units.....calling them to active duty. The President told them they'd have time to go home.....take care of business....say goodbye, and then they were heading to Camp Blanding in Florida for a year. "Heavy duty training," Ray says. Getting them ready to go to war.

Camp Shelby, Mississippi
June 1942
Ray Perkins unit moved there, for further training, after Camp Blanding.
Photo: Courtesy Ray Perkins

February 1941, Ray headed south, for his year in the Florida sun. He was on guard duty at Camp Blanding, December 7^{th,} of 41. "Came in...turned on the radio and I heard the President say Pearl Harbor had been hit. I got a pretty good idea I wasn't going to be going home." He was right.

He did get a short leave, before his unit was moved to Mississippi and then to Louisiana. They sighted in....got familiar with their new guns. Next stop the Pacific and the war.

He landed in New Zealand; "A few days"...was transferred to New Caledonia, "To get equipped. That'd be the last peaceful place before we went into combat." Banguna, an island in the New Georgia group, "They sent us there to drive the Japanese out." Battery "B" out of Brewer and a company of Marines went into Bangona. The Maine guys did their job. Japanese troops fled.

The Maine folks pretty much stayed together while Ray was in the South Pacific, hopping from island to island....places with unfamiliar names like New Georgia... Guadalcanal, "Our whole thing during the war was backing up the 103rd Infantry which is the Maine National Guard. We'd (*artillery*) be behind them. I always gave a lot of credit to the infantry because in the artillery you're back two or three miles.....you're not bayonet to bayonet, unless they break through." Ray's job as machine gunner was to protect the big guns and keep the enemy from breaking through. They never did.

He draws a pretty clear picture of what our folks went through over there. "You didn't get any more hot meals. You ate jungle rations. They had a little can of Vienna sausage, a little can of biscuits, two or three pieces of candy and four cigarettes.....every meal we got had four cigarettes in it. The temperature in the daytime would be 120 degrees. Every night, just before dark it would rain. Everything you had was soaking wet. It might cool down to 95 degrees at night." That didn't matter because, "You never did get a night's sleep. There wasn't a night the Japanese didn't send down...anywhere from two to a dozen planes to drop a few bombs."

He says he waited for letters from home. His girlfriend, he gave her a diamond just before he left.....she wrote to him every day he was there. They'd go for weeks without mail. "The letters came in bunches."

Ray also got terrible news while he was fighting in the South Pacific. The Chaplain called him in. "He says I got bad news. I just got word your father has been killed." Ray worried about his mother and sisters running the farm. "I had to forget that because within two weeks I was right back in combat." He continued to fight even though he caught malaria. That's what got him.

The malaria....the loss of weight and his last night in combat on Do Ke Doke Island, "I can remember it plainly. I was standing out in the open without a helmet on. I wasn't afraid any more. One of my friends grabbed me and put me back into a protected area." The next morning

Cologne 2000:
This picture of the Cologne (Koln) cathedral was taken during the "Blackhawk" tour in 2000. The railroad bridge was destroyed during WW II. Blackhawk Division Photo

The twin spires of the historic "Dom" dominate the skyline of Cologne. Construction on the cathedral began in the thirteenth century. It received minor damage during WW II, but has since been restored.

For several days, the "Blackhawks" defended the west bank of the Rhine, from Cologne to Bonn....about a 23 mile front. They turned back several probes by German patrols.

"We were moved down the Rhine...where we crossed at Remagen....went over on the other side and then came back up into the Ruhr valley....a manufacturing area." Randolph didn't know it at the time, but his regiment was part of an allied ring that circled the entire region. Just days later, the Ruhr region would fall and more than three hundred thousand enemy troops would be taken prisoner........the largest mass surrender of German troops during the war. "We were looking for prisoners and we got um."

Remagen:
The 86th crossed the Rhine at Remagen on a pontoon bridge.
Photo: U.S.Army

Quickly, the 86th moved out, linking up with elements of the 9th Army, splitting the German forces. They captured the cities of Attendorn, Luderscheid and Hagen, essentially cutting off further attack from German forces.

By mid April, the 86th was moved to Southern Germany, to assist General Patton's 3rd Army. Adams remembers it well. "I remember seeing Patton several times.....General Patton we called him, and many other things. He was a tough S.O.B.....the general impression was, with the pearl handled pistols, he was putting on a front, but he was a leader.....and he was out there."

The division moved down into Bavaria, where Hitler said the German Reich would make a final stand.

The 86th headed Patton's 3rd Army advance through Bavaria. In sixteen days they covered 110 miles, crossed six major rivers, and took the cities of Ansback, Ingolstadt, Freising and Oberdorf.

By early May when the Germans surrendered, the 86th Infantry Division had participated in three major battles, the Rhine, the Ruhr Pocket and Bavaria. Randolph had been in the war just two months.

It wasn't over for him though. He didn't have enough time…enough points, to be discharged, so it was back to the states......a short leave......off to school for retraining....and then board a ship for the war in the Pacific. "We were out to sea about five or six days when the atomic bomb was dropped. They shipped us down to the Philippines where we were in a mop-up operation. A few of us went into the hills and chased 'Japs' but most of um were coming in......surrendering. That's about the end of it."

Today, as he looks back at the war, "I felt it was our duty to be there. The Germans were a bunch of.......the things that they did over there to other races, like the Jewish boys are beyond comprehension. I felt that we were much needed, and that we did a good job."

Randolph came home and attended college on the "GI Bill." He taught school in Limestone and Lincoln for a few years, and then became a company representative for a Brewer chemical company, until he retired.

Randolph and Ida, "a Howland girl" were married in August of 1949. They raised four daughters.

WORLD WAR II

Bangor, Maine,
The crew of a B-17 poses in front of their plane at Dow
Field during WW II.
You can see the "Good Luck" graffiti all over the plane.
Photo: Richard Shaw

NORMA TEWKSBURY OOGHE

Stonington, Maine

U.S. Navy – Waves..................February 1943 – December 1945

Administration

"I decided to go, to do my part."

WHAT PAY DOES A NAVY WAVE GET?

RATE	Monthly Base Pay–Clear	Food Allowance*	Quarters Allowance*	Total Monthly Income
Apprentice Seaman	$50.00	$54.00	$37.50	$141.50
Seaman Second Class	54.00	54.00	37.50	145.50
Seaman First Class	66.00	54.00	37.50	157.50
Petty Officers	78.00 TO 126.00	54.00	37.50	169.50 TO 217.50

*[Unless food and quarters are provided by Navy]

PLUS $200. for clothing, the finest medical and dental care, special tax exemption, low-cost Government life insurance, and free mail, reduced rates on transportation, theater tickets, etc.

US Navy recruiting poster.
Photo: US Navy

After the bombing of Pearl Harbor, the Navy was facing a shortage of men for all duties. The Secretary of the Navy petitioned the Congress for a women's reserve. In July of 1942, the Navy Women's Reserve Act was passed. The organization's official name became "Women Accepted for Volunteer Emergency Service" or "Waves." The word emergency was used intentionally to indicate the temporary nature of the women's service. It turned out it wasn't. By 1945 there were more than 84,000 women in the Navy.

Norma Ooghe joined the Waves soon after the service was created. She was the first woman from Stonington to sign up and among the first from the state.

She had completed Becker College and was working at Eastern Maine General Hospital in Bangor. On days off, when she went home to Stonington, "They'd drive me down in the ambulance."

231

WORLD WAR II

Bangor, WWII
A group of women prepare to leave for training in the
Woman's Army Auxiliary Corps. at Daytona Beach, Fl.
Estimates vary, but by most accounts, more than 300,000
women served in military and nurse services roles during
WW II.
Millions more stayed home, raised families, assembled
bombs, and built the boats, planes and other implements of
war.
Photo: Courtesy Anne McNeil McCarthy

THOMAS NEWMAN

South West Harbor, Maine

U.S. Army.....September 1944 – August 1946

Private, Infantry

"By this time tomorrow, some of you might not be alive."

Tom Newman walked across Europe. "I rode on the outside of one of Patton's tanks one afternoon, but other than that, I walked." From outside Luxembourg to Lazne, Czechoslovakia...he walked....and fought...and survived the cold.

Tom's a Southwest Harbor boy, although there weren't many boys left, by the time he graduated from high school. "I think there were twenty-three or twenty-four boys who started the freshman class. When we graduated, there were six of us left." The war had the rest.

Tom Newman at home in S.W. Harbor, December 1944
Photo: Courtesy Tom Newman

The war would get Tom pretty soon, too. "I knew I had to go anyway. They had the draft." He had already received his draft notice. Tom turned eighteen on June 4th, 1944. He graduated from high school on June 6th, D-Day, and in August he signed up for the Army. "I tried to get in the Navy, but they wouldn't take me. They said I was color blind."

Tom was assigned to the 30th Division when he first arrived in Europe. "I caught up with them at about the middle of the "Battle of the Bulge;" about mid-January, 1945. According to "Army Ground Forces," Fact Sheets prepared at the end of the war, when German Field Marshall Von Runstedt attempted his breakthrough in December 1944, to capture Antwerp, the 30th gave his troops such a mauling, that the Germans called the Division, "Roosevelt's SS Troops."

He was in Chemitz, Czechoslovakia when the war ended, although a letter he wrote to his parents indicates he didn't know it was over, right away.

"May 6, 1945

"Dear Mom Dad & Family,

There's been a lot of good news lately hasn't there? I don't see how it can last much longer. The sooner it get's over the better for everyone.

There was a kid here in my company who I chummed with a lot. He was a great guy. He was killed a little while back. Sure miss the guy. He was really swell. I was only a short distance from him when he got hit. Things like that really build you a temper."

Tom's letter went on to tell his folks he was feeling fine...not nervous during battle. He said he got mad when the Germans were firing at him and he didn't know where they were.

In spite of the shooting, he remembered Mother's Day.

"I want to wish you a very Happy Mother's Day and wish I could be there to do more than just wish. I sent you $16.10 for the occasion and don't spend it all in one place." That was last month's pay for me."

Good night now. Loads of Love, Tommy"

Tom came home after the war and went back to O.E. Harper trucking until 1948, when he went back into the Army again. He was part of the coast patrol, assigned to Fort Williams in Cape Elizabeth.

"They were destroying shells. They'd dump the powder out and burn it. In fact some of um; after a while their hair even turned green, because of the sulfur or whatever was in those shells." Tom stood guard a lot. He says Cape Elizabeth was good duty.

He got out of the Army again, just as the Korean War was beginning…in 1950…..went back to trucking, hauling seafood…..had owned his own company for thirty-seven years when he retired in 1992. His son runs the company now.

The Kiwanis and American Legion keep Tom busy these days, "I put a lot of time in both of those." He has a big garden in the summer.

In January of 2007, when I talked to him for this book, he had gotten home from helping with preparations for a dinner, that night at the Legion Hall.

The next night when I tried to reach him, he was in Bangor supporting the high school basketball team.

Eighty years old…he's retired, but you'd never know it.

Tom Newman at the American Legion Hall in S.W. Harbor, May 2006
Photo: Courtesy Tom Newman

attack, like so many others, he couldn't stand by: "Got all patriotic after Pearl Harbor," he says, and so he closed his practice, cleaned out his office and signed up.

Daniels tried for the Air Force first, but couldn't make the grade on the eye test, so he turned to the Army. A graduate doctor today would automatically receive a commission; most become captains, and are assigned to a medical unit as doctors. The Army didn't recognize Osteopathic Medicine in 1942, so Daniels thought he was going to become a "Tanker."

Well, wrong again. The Army assigned him to Company B, 75th Medical Battalion of the 5th Armored Division. Doctor William Daniels, was to spend his days with one of the fightingest divisions in the war, as an enlisted medic.

Looking back he says, "I'll tell you one thing, it was a hell of an experience."

The "Siegfried Line" was a German defensive line of bunkers, tunnels and tank traps that stretched from the border of the Netherlands to Switzerland.

Map: Courtesy-Wikipedia

For those of us who served in the military during peacetime...I guess for anyone who wasn't there, it's hard to imagine the horrible reality of combat. Daniels remembers a September day in 1944, near Aachenon, on the "Siegfried Line."

In late August of 1944, Hitler ordered the reconstruction of the Siegfried Line, as a last-ditch attempt to reverse the course of the war. Daniels says, "We got on the Siegfried Line, and I had one long day.

I got shot at. A sniper missed my head by about two inches. They killed a buddy next to me."

He was near the Elbe River in Germany when he crossed paths with another Mainer......a badly wounded, fellow Mainer. Daniels noticed the man's nametag: "Daigle." "Ft Kent, Maine?" he asked. "How'd you know?" Abel Daigle replied. Daniels told him he was from Maine too, and with the name Daigle, Fort Kent is a pretty good bet. At that point Daigle's lapsed into unconsciousness.

Daniels treated him and he was taken away to a hospital. For the next 39 years, Daniels wondered what had happened to Able Daigle. He feared perhaps he didn't survive.

Bangor Daily News: August 10, 1984.
Galen Cole, in the center, also a 5th Armored Veteran, looks on as Able Daigle, on the left and Doctor William Daniels remembers a day in 1945 during WW II. All three were attending the reunion of the 5th armored division.
   Photo: Carroll Hall, courtesy of the Bangor Daily News.

WORLD WAR I

Bangor, June 29, 1918
More than 1,200 Nurses parade down Central Street in a
benefit parade for the Penobscot Chapter of the American
Red Cross.
The Nurses played an important role, both at home and
abroad, during World War I.
Photo: Dick Shaw

DONALD COLLINS

Caribou, Maine

U.S. Army.............December 31, 1943 – January 19, 1946

Sergeant, Infantry

"At that time, I thought, I'm darned glad it's over."

The Collins family arrived in Aroostook County, before the town of Caribou arrived. Today, the S.W. Collins Company, hardware and building materials center is one of Caribou's most successful businesses.

Samuel Collins started it all in 1844. He was part of the crowd that answered a state challenge to develop and populate Aroostook County. After the northern boundary with Canada was finally settled, the state created a program that would provide acres of land for anyone who would move to "the county" and open a lumber mill and a grist mill. The mills had to be operated for at least two years. Although they no longer cut lumber, or grind flour, the S.W. Collins Company is still there, in the same location. Incidentally, Caribou wasn't incorporated as a town until April 5, 1859; fifteen years later.

That's the solid background that sent Donald Collins off to war, a century later.

Reim, France May 7, 1945

German General Alfred Jodl, signs the documents of unconditional German Surrender at General Eisenhower's Hq.
The surrender ended WW II hostilities in Europe.

Photo: U.S. National Archives

Wetzlar, Germany, March 29, 1945
Allied soldiers pose by signs they erected at a POW camp, as they were being freed. Allied forces freed our guys, as they moved across Europe.
Photo: National Archives

CHARLES A. FLANAGAN

Bangor, Maine

U.S. Army.........December 11, 1942 – Killed in Action

Private First Class, Infantry

"Charlie did a lot in his short life."

The telegram arrived December 17, 1944. "John P. Flanagan, 207 Maple St, Bangor, Maine: the Secretary of War asks that I assure you of his deep sympathy in the loss of your son, Private First Class Charles A. Flanagan. Report now states he was killed in action twenty five November in Germany...Letter follows. Dunlop Acting the Adjutant General"

"Charlie did a lot in his short life," his brother Tom says, "and he meant a lot to a lot of people. Charlie was one of those Maple Street boys in Bangor; industrious... enterprising... good kids; two years older than Tom. "I remember something that happened when he was in the third grade. We went home to lunch every day. When we arrived home, Ma would often send Charlie to the store on Mount Hope Avenue for a loaf of bread." Tom recalls, "One day she sent him to Collins market. He went out the door and in ten seconds he was back with the bread and a big smile. He had figured what was going to happen, and had stopped on his way home and had hidden the bread on the front porch."

Charlie Flanagan during a visit to Camp, Lee,1943. Photo: Courtesy Tom Flanagan

Tom says, "Charlie was a builder, long before the days of electric drills, "Skil" saws and home centers." Charlie got scrap lumber from Ervin Brooks Mill on Mt. Hope Avenue... ten cents for an armload...five cents

251

The Army shows Charlie's date of death as November 25th, but his brother Tom says, "That's wrong." Historical records of the 84th report "A lull settled on the battlefield," on the 25th.

In the spring of 1945, Tom went to Margraten Cemetery to find Charlie's grave. Records there listed him from the 102nd Division. The 102nd was on the left flank of the 84th. He had been reported missing for a few days before his parents were notified of his death. Tom thinks, "It seems likely that he fell on the 23rd of November at the age of 21 years and 6 months. *(Charlie's family has since brought him home for burial.)*

One of Charlie's last letters home, in late 1944, contained a request to use ten or fifteen dollars of his money to buy a wedding present for his friends Galen and Sue Cole. Sue and Galen had been married on September 17th.

In 1997 when Galen decided to construct a memorial to World War II, on the grounds of the Cole Land Transportation Museum in Bangor, his boyhood friend Charlie Flanigan was his choice for the bronze monument.

Lowell Kjenstad, Galen's friend and employee who helped design, build and create the museum suggested the WW II jeep. All services used jeeps for 'Land Transportation.' That's a sculptured likeness of Charlie in the driver's seat. Galen says, "He'd give his life in a moment for our country's freedom. That's the kind of man Charlie was. He was our only choice for the monument."

Maine State World War II Memorial, Bangor
Dedicated by Governor Angus King on October 11, 1997.
Photo: Cole Museum

THOMAS S. FLANAGAN

Portland, Me

U.S. Army....June 1943 – November 1945

Sgt, Graves Registration Company

"It was terrible."

First of all, I was in the military during peacetime. I admit I don't know what I'm talking about, but I think if I were in WW II, I would rather have been in the infantry than to have Tom Flanagan's job.

Tom's a Bangor boy....graduated from Bangor High School in 1943. A month later he was in the Army. When he reported to the armory for his physical, an orthopedic doctor who had treated him for a foot injury spotted him. "He ordered a special X-ray," and then stamped Tom's record, 'Limited Service.' "I was not pleased," he says.

Processing and training took him to Massachusetts, Camp Lee in Virginia, and then Camp Reynolds near Sharon,

Private Tom Flanagan
Camp Lee, Virginia
September 1943
Photo: Courtesy Tom Flanagan

Pennsylvania. While he was there, he went on a bus to Youngstown, Ohio; to a dance for soldiers. "I spent some time talking with a local girl. At the end of the evening, she told him, "This has been fun, but don't tell me your name or address, and I won't tell you mine.' She then explained that she had met a soldier and liked him. He went overseas. She sent him brownies and they were returned to her, marked 'deceased."

June 2nd, 1944 he headed across the ocean....four days before "D-Day." "We learned about it on the ship. They came around and had a moment of silence."

These days, "Three days a week I'm on Dialysis, from six o'clock in the morning until eleven. That kind of bums me out for the rest of the day."

"I do some wood working and I have eight children and eighteen grandchildren. They keep me busy."

Tom was part of the 'Graves' unit from August 1944 until June 1945. "It's a very tough job. People get sort of conditioned to it." He admits he still thinks about it.

Portland, Maine October 2006
Tom Flanagan and Quilla Flanagan Burt, his granddaughter.
Photo: Courtesy Tom Flanagan

GEORGE C. BENJAMIN

Auburn, Maine

U.S. Army...........................June 12, 1939 – July 31, 1969

Colonel, Armor

"You see heroes every single day."

George Benjamin rode horses with Eleanor Roosevelt.

Isn't that just like an old reporter? Here we have a man who served an honorable, decorated thirty-year career in the Army, retired as a full "Bird" Colonel, fought in five WW II campaigns in Europe, and I begin his story, talking about a couple of months before WW II.

You have to admit though; it is unique.

In reality, horses have played an important part in most of George Benjamin's life. He got that from George Cobb, a country veterinarian in Housatonic, Massachusetts; George's grandfather. "He was a real hero of mine," he says. Cobb had horses....big work horses......George was around those a lot, and he cleaned stables for Eben Kimbal, "just down the road," who had riding horses. He got to ride for free.

It was only natural then, that when he went to Massachusetts State College; we now know it as the University of Massachusetts ...only natural that when he got there, he would become a member of the "ROTC" Horse Cavalry program. His completed his pre-med studies, but in the end, the horses and military training for or combat, won out over medicine.

Berlin, Germany 1947
Lt. Col. George Benjamin, Commanding Officer of the 16th Constabulary Squadron
Photo: Courtesy George Benjamin

Colonel George C. Benjamin
He was 88 years old when this picture was taken at the
Cole Museum in Bangor, in 2004.
Photo: Courtesy Col. George Benjamin

CARROLL FRYE

Eddington, Maine

U.S. Army-Air Force....................February 1943 – November 1945

Sergeant, Aircraft Mechanic/Gunner

"We dropped bombs on Cologne and Hamburg and destructed those two cities."

"We weren't too bad off."

That's how Carroll Frye describes the war years for his family. He was an only child and lived on a farm in Bradley. His dad worked at a woolen company. "We had a cow, chickens and ducks....stuff like that. Life was a lot simpler."

Carroll signed up for a National Youth Organization program when he graduated from Old Town high school. He learned aircraft maintenance at the airport in Houlton, through the Civil Air Patrol.

When he enlisted in the Army-Air Force, he was ready. The air force gave him additional training as a propeller specialist.

The 8th Air Force, in Europe, got him first, as a crew chief and machine gunner on a B-17. Carroll was flying overhead as the troops fought their way ashore at Normandy. He told me he saw it all. "We had to drop a few bombs and scatter the people *(enemy forces)* behind the lines." His plane also towed gliders over the cliffs to transport U.S. troops behind the enemy lines, to soften the resistance for the troops coming ashore.

Soon after Normandy, Carroll transferred to the 436th troop carrier group in the 9th Air Force and from B-17's to C-47s.... the "Gooney Bird."

The C-47 "Gooney Bird" was a work horse during WW II and Korea. They were used as gun-ships during the Vietnam War.
More than 10,000 were produced.
Some are still flying today.
Photo:Wikipedia Foundation

265

They dropped supplies to the 82nd and 101st Airborne, the "Screaming Eagles" at the "Battle of Bastogne."

Europe
December 1944
101st Airborne troops retrieving air dropped supplies during the siege of Bastogne.
Photo: U.S. Army

Carroll says the destruction he saw below them was unbelievable. "We dropped bombs on Cologne and Hamburg and destructed those two cities. We couldn't do any different because they put their ammunition dumps and all the men and supplies close to churches and schools. As far as I could see, it was practically demolished."

He was impressed with the spirit of the people, particularly the French. "They cooperated and worked hard and were ready to put their life on the line at any time."

Carroll worked at the A & P and tried the insurance business for a few years after he got out. He eventually got his engineer's license and went to work at Bangor Mental Health Institute taking charge of the boilers and maintenance needs.

Looking back at the war, "I'd do it all over." Carroll told me.

Carroll Frye in late 1945, just before he was discharged.

Photo: Courtesy Carroll Frye

WW II RECRUITING POSTER

"I Want You" recruiting poster.
Artist James Montgomery used himself as a model for this poster. It was originally published in the July 6, 1916 edition of "Leslie's Weekly" magazine, and used extensively for recruiting in WW I. It was revived for WW II.
Photo: National Archives

RAYMOND EDWARD VEAR

U.S. ARMY.................August 1943 – April 1946

Corporal, Infantry

"You're scared all the time you're in combat."

Ray Vear was five feet eight inches tall and jumped center for his Winslow High School basketball team. Like everything else he tried, he did it well. People who knew Ray say his heart was at least seven feet tall.

Ray was born in Winslow on May 22nd of 1926. He told me he didn't know what English was until he got to school. His father, Ovide, came to Winslow from Canada. Laura, his mom moved south from Aroostook County. They only spoke French at home.

Ray talked to the Navy...ended up in the Army...drafted. After basic in the summer heat at Camp Blanding near Jacksonville, Florida, and a few weeks at school for training in intelligence and reconnaissance, Ray headed to Europe and the war. The little guy with the big heart would find himself in the thick of things very quickly.

Ray Vear home on leave before heading for the war.
Photo: Courtesy Marilyn Lavelle

Ray received his assignment to General Patton's 3rd army. He was assigned to the 4th Armored Division, Company a, 10th Armored Infantry Battalion.

"The first day in combat was the most scariest day I ever spent in my life." Ray said. There were body parts everywhere. There was always someone being killed.

He was dug in at the front. He spotted several guys he knew. They were dug in a few yards away. Ray started in their direction, "I took two steps out of that fox hole and a shell blew up amongst um, and killed them all. I dove right back in the fox hole and wouldn't move."

269

His unit was always on the attack. Ray spent days under fire. "You're scared all the time you're in combat. The people who tell you they're not scared are full of baloney."

It would only get worse. Ray would be a part of one of the most controversial missions of the war. To this day, historians believe it was a suicide mission wrongly ordered by General George S. Patton, Jr.

Patton's son-in-law, Lieutenant Colonel John Waters had been taken prisoner by the Germans and was being held at a prisoner of war camp at Hammelburg.

Lt. Gen. George S Patton Jr.
He was known as "Old Blood and Guts" after a reporter misquoted him when he said it takes blood and brains to win a war.
Photo: US Army

March 25th...Patton's forces had just crossed the Rhine River. They were eighty miles from the POW camp. Patton wrote to his wife Beatrice, "Hope to send an expedition tomorrow to get John."

Even today historians are not in agreement with Patton's motives. Putting his men in such danger to rescue his son-in-law seems merciless, and even beyond Patton's well-known egotistical self-centeredness.

On the night of March 25th, 1945, Captain Abe Baum was assigned to lead a task force to free the U.S. officers being held at the Hammelburg POW camp.

There was a company of armored infantry, a company of Sherman tanks plus a platoon of light tanks, a platoon of assault guns and a recon platoon. The bulk of "Task Force Baum" would be the twenty-seven half tracks. A small force, to move fast…. sneak through the German lines; fifty-three vehicles, carrying 294 men, to free Colonel Waters and the other prisoners and return with them.

The mission unexpectedly bogged down as it began. The 37th tank battalion and 10th armored were commanded to clear the half mile long main street of Schweinheim so that "Task Force Baum" could dash through. It didn't happen.

They found themselves facing stiff resistance from German units reinforced by cadets and staff from the 'SS Officer Candidate' school at Aschaffenburg. A panzerfaust knocked out the first tank in the column, blocking the street.

The Baum task force would get through but the quick passage, instead, would take hours. Ray says the whole trip to the POW camp was just like that. They had hoped to be there by morning, but they had only reached the main river at Gemunden, still miles from the POW camp.

Ray said he learned there were three German divisions after them. By afternoon they reached the town of Hammelburg, still a couple of miles from the POW camp. Once again German resistance was fierce. A German unit equipped with 88mm antitank guns, had hidden in the railroad station and was ready for the Americans. "Task Force Baum" took more heavy casualties.

Resistance at the POW camp was lighter but the battle raged on there too, until German General von Goeckel, the camp commander realized their resistance was futile and wanted to give up. It was John Waters, Patton's son-in-law, who volunteered to contact the Americans. He and four others went outside the camp to deliver the German's surrender message. They took with them an American flag and a white flag made from a bed sheet.

A "Baum Task Force" soldier stepped out just as they were coming out the gate. Waters shouted "amerikaner!" just as the soldier fired.

The bullet hit waters below the right hip. The wound was so bad he would be hospitalized and couldn't be moved. The task force, which came to free him, would have to leave him behind.

"Task Force Baum" was small when it started the mission, but by now it was a shadow of itself. Many of the tanks and other vehicles had been lost. Their gas was all used up. "We had nothing left to fight back with," Ray told me. About a third of the men had been either wounded or killed and they were surrounded. "All hell broke loose," as they tried to leave, he remembers. They were in trouble.

Captain Baum realizing their situation was hopeless, ordered all the wounded left in a large barn at a nearby farm. He hoped the Germans would care for them. Ray remembered Baum, "crouched beneath some trees with a map showing us where to go….and how to get out of there." Baum told them to get back to the lines the best way they could.

Ray and five other headed out. They had a single pistol between them. They walked at night and hid in bushes as German patrols came by.

They hid and walked for three days. They found raw sugar beets in a farmer's field and ate them….but they were hungry and tired and decided to go to a nearby town to look for food and a chance to rest. Many of the houses in the town were bombed out, but they found one on the outskirts that had all kinds of food….all kinds of canned goods……pumpernickel bread. "We were in seventh heaven," Ray said, "We were getting warmed up and getting food in our stomachs. We ate like crazy." They spent the night in the house.

The next morning as they prepared to leave they heard voices outside….a man and two women. When one of the women came in to check the house, they grabbed her, but the two still outside called for help and within minutes the house was surrounded. They had chosen the Burgermeister's house….the mayor's house. German troops were already nearby.

His German captors took him to a schoolhouse at first. Ray remembers, "Our guard was drunker'n a skunk." From there he was marched……taken by train…..and then marched more, to a POW camp at Moosberg. He would spend 33 days in captivity….until may 8th when American troops stormed through the main gate of the prison and freed him. Even in much later life, Ray choked up as he remembered the day.

Ray was extraordinarily proud of his military years, but I think he liked the years after the war more, teaching and coaching…. "Helping kids."

Center Drive School, Orrington
"Ray Vear Day" He loved being called "Coach."
Photo: Courtesy Marilyn Lavelle

He was the first principal at Monroe Elementary School. He taught history and social studies at Waterville High School for more than twenty-five years. Ray coached baseball, basketball and football in Waterville, Winslow and Orrington for over fifty years. The kids gave Ray the nickname "Pop."

In addition to teaching and coaching, Ray was announcer at Winslow High School football games for more than thirty years.

At his death in January of 2006, Ray was a volunteer at the Cole Museum in Bangor. He participated in the "Veteran Interview Program." He was still, "Helping kids."

RAYMOND EDWARD VEAR
May 22, 1926 – January 18, 2006

Excerpts from "Two Maine High School Boys – Two Men of War" Cole Museum 2006

He likes talking with the young students. "They haven't the faintest idea in the world, what it was like in the World War Two era, here in the United States. They can't understand it was the difference between the entire country backing the war effort and doing everything they could, compared to today."

WW II Ration Stamps.
Things like meat, sugar, butter, coffee, shoes, clothing and gasoline were rationed during the war. Bread, milk and beer were not.
Photo: Zach S. Henderson Library
            Georgia Southern University

He tells the students about when Catherine and he got married. "They don't understand that sugar was rationed. My mother and my wife's mother put their *(ration)* stamps for sugar together, so that we could have a wedding cake."

They must have gotten the ingredients right! That was August, 1944. In 2006 Catherine and Earl celebrated their sixty-second anniversary.

Earl and Kay Kingsbury at home in January 2007
Photo: Ron Murray

WALLY LaFOUNTAIN

Winslow, Maine

U.S. Army.........September 1944 – June 1946

Corporal, Infantry

"I guess I have to tell you I'm a little scared."

There were eighty-nine students in Wally LaFountain's class when he started high school in Woodstock, Vermont. Thirty-two graduated. The rest were already fighting the war.

Wally had signed up before he graduated too. "That was the thing to do in those days." He turned eighteen in August of 1944, and in September he headed south for Army basic training.

He was the youngest of five children, on their Vermont farm. "We were poor...everyone was poor." Even here at home, the war influenced every part of life. "Everything was beginning to be rationed."

Wally LaFountain
Basic training
picture, 1944
Photo: Courtesy
Wally LaFountain

The allies were on the offensive by the fall of 1944. The 28th Infantry Division entered combat in World War Two, on July 22, 1944, landing on the beaches of Normandy. Combat was nothing new for the 28th.

287

WORLD WAR II

Washington, D.C., August 14, 1945
President Harry S. Truman announces the Japanese
surrender.
Photo: Abbie Rowe, National Park Service

JAMES M. ALDRICH

Deer Isle, Maine

U.S. Army-Air Force.......November 1943 – November 1945

2nd Lieutenant, Navigator

"The most boring year of my life I think,"

James Aldrich was living in Providence. Rhode Island when he got the call to report for aviation training. He had volunteered. That helped him avoid the infantry. His family was in transit when he got the call. James's father, Norman, had been a 2nd Lt. in a machine gun company during World War One. James says, his dad saw the Second World War coming so he went back in, 'to see if he could help.' His dad was assigned Base Adjutant at the prisoner or war holding facility in Houlton, Maine.

Nashua, New Hampshire, 1944
James Aldrich preparing for flight.
Photo: Courtesy James Aldrich

James started his training in aviation in New Hampshire. He made another stop in San Marcos, Texas for navigator training on B-24's. The focus was on "BTO".... "Bombing Through the Overcast".....radar bombing. Radar was becoming more useful, "and to a navigator it was a God send." The Navy invented the term "RADAR" in 1941.

Technically, the Army Air Force was only a year and a half old when James Aldrich came on board. Oh, it had a much longer history than that. It was way back in January of 1905 when the federal government had an offer from two Dayton, Ohio inventors to provide the government with a lighter than air flying machine.

humanity goes wrong, this is what happens." He stopped…thought about it, "How to avoid going to war is a difficult matter, when such guides as the "golden rule" and "turning the other cheek" hardly do the job. Too often turning the other cheek actually means closing your eyes."

Deer Isle, November 2006   James Aldrich at his Deer Isle home.
Photo: Courtesy James Aldrich

WILLARD PRIOR-CROFOOT

Blue Hill, Maine

U.S. Army-Air Force..January 19, 1943 – November 27, 1945

Corporal-Technician, Aircraft Maintenance

"I saw him walking up toward the prop."

Things were pretty snarled up in January of 1943. The country had been thrust into a two-theatre war. We were scrambling to catch up with manpower, supplies and equipment.

That's why Bill Crofoot had the experience so many others had. He thought he was going to be assigned in one direction and ended up in another.

He enlisted at age seventeen......his dad signed for him. He thought he was headed for the Air Force, but the military had another idea. After Army basic training, Bill was sent on to Ranger training. It was pretty tough he says, "I had to go over a forty foot rope, hand over hand, no feet, with a 85 pound field pack and a eight pound rifle." He made it, but the course of his career changed again.

**Paris, Tennessee-
Summer 1943**
Bill Crofoot suited up
for Ranger training.
Photo: Courtesy Bill
Crofoot

Someone in authority had noticed that Bill recorded a pretty high mechanical aptitude on his tests. At that point the military was shorter on aircraft mechanics than rangers. It's a pretty well known fact that it takes eight or nine people on the ground for every crewmember flying a plane.

Bill was diverted to Army-Air Force aircraft maintenance school....and the rest, as the saying goes, "is history,".......well, sort of. He did go to aircraft maintenance school, and then on to advance training at a Royal Air Force facility in England and ended up with the 374th Air Service Squadron just outside Paris, France.

His arrival there became a bit of a footnote in French history.

"Everybody was there to greet the troops coming in." Bill says. He was manning a fire extinguisher by one of their planes when he spotted a small boy heading for the spinning propeller on another of the B-26s. "I saw him walking up toward the prop....I didn't know how to speak French at all." Bill dropped the fire extinguisher, "I grabbed the kid and took him back away from there." He saved the boy's life.

Paris during WW II: (Left) General Charles de Gaulle reviews French troops. (Right) Willard Crofoot's 1963 invitation to review Bastille Day activities with President de Gaulle.
Photo: Pierre LaFranc, La France dans La guerre – Invitation: Courtesy Bill Crofoot

French officials expressed their appreciation....he was even invited to dinner at the mayor's house. The incident was pretty much filed away, until Bill returned to France on vacation in 1963. When officials learned he was there, they remembered his quick action during the war and decided special attention was in order. He got it, in the form of an invitation to stand beside French President Charles de Gaulle to review the Bastille Day parade. "I had to look up at him. He was a big tall guy."

It was a big job to keep the planes in the air, during the war. They took quite a beating. Bill says we just kept patching them up. In fact, he was assigned to the maintenance crew of a B-26 that earned the nickname "Patches" it received so many hits. Ground crews counted 264 holes from shrapnel on one single mission over St Omer. Bill, the other mechanics and the sheet metal men patched the planes up and sent them back up again. He says one time they had to take the front from one damaged plane, the rear from another and put them together.

France 1944
Bill Crofoot and team make one B-26 out of two.
Photo: Courtesy Bill Crofoot

Bill was also one of the guys called on to get badly needed supplies and fuel to General Patton's forces during the "Battle of the Bulge." Patton's 3rd Army was racing across Europe faster than the German blitzkrieg. The offensive, however, came to a screeching halt as the Third Army literally ran out of gas near the Moselle River just outside Metz, Franch. Bill's convoy raced through the German lines and delived the desperately needed gasoline.

Bill says the troops he saw along the way were experiencing terrible conditions. "Your hands, your feet were frozen. It was ice cold.....snowy. Sometimes they would sleep together to keep warm....they'd be in a fox hole....so they could keep each other warm."

Scotty was sick and missed being a "plank owner" but he made sea trials. There were almost three thousand men on board the Franklin, "Big Ben." "There were men on there, I never knew…just too many people. He was an engineer, down in the boiler room..part of "The black gang."

The Franklin arrived in the Pacific in time for the later stages of the Marianas operation. From late June into September, her planes conducted strikes on targets in the Bonins, Marianas, and the Carolines.

She was damaged by a Japanese attack in mid 1944. "The first bomb hit the deck "H" elevator." That killed 18 men.

October 30, 1944, The Franklin (R) and the USS Belleau Wood on fire after "Kamikaze" attacks. Both were operating off the Philippines. A second "Kamikaze" plane missed the Franklin and hit the Belleau Woods.
Photo: US Navy

A Japanese "Kamikaze" suicide plane hit her in late October. "He hit aft of the main island…went down through the flight deck and exploded on the hanger deck." They lost fifty-six men in that attack.

Each time, repairs were made and 'Big Ben' returned to the fight. She was off shore, when our troops went ashore on Guam, Okinawa and the Philippines.

By March 19, 1945, the Franklin had joined the Fifth fleet, operating just seventy-six miles off the Japanese mainland. She was hit again. This time, it was bad…very, very bad.

Scotty remembers the morning, well, "I had just got in my bunk when I heard the first bomb go off. It was two decks above me." The first of many explosions. "I heard somebody hollering, and a guy came through the hatch, he said 'Scotty get your shoes on, lets get the hell out of here."

Smoke was already filling the passage ways. "I heard somebody else. The guy was screaming...he was coming toward us. He came through the hatch and he fell right beside us. He was dead."

The man had been just two compartments away. "Shrapnel had come through the bulkhead. It hit him in the stomach and the ankles. I couldn't figure out how he got as far as he did."

March 19, 1945
The USS Franklin is said to have received the most severe damage and was the most highly decorated ship to survive in WW II.
Photo: Naval War College

More explosions shook the carrier. "By that time, people were running into our compartment, coming aft...quite a few people."

The Chief Petty Officer came in and told them to close the hatch. "We dogged it down. Now we're locked in and we're down three decks. That thing is still blowing up in good shape." Bombs and ammunition was stored just a deck above them.

Scotty was standing by the hatch. "I heard somebody scratching on the hatch...out where the smoke was." Scotty was standing next to Leonard Hall, a 1st Class water tender. "I said, let's let him in Leonard."

The Chief ordered them not open the hatch. "What we said was, in nice language, was to hell with that, and we opened the hatch."

Brooklyn Navy Yard, 1945
Ernest Scott, Edward Carlisle and Harold Smith, all Baileyville residents, were reunited after the war.
Edward Carlisle died six years after this photograph was taken.
Photo: Courtesy "Paper Talks" magazine.

"It was Eddie Carlisle, a guy I grew up with, and went to school with. He was trying to find a way out, like everybody else." Scotty says, "He wasn't hurt, but he couldn't see. He couldn't breath too good."

They made up their minds, "We just had to get out of there. We couldn't stay there until it went over." Once again the Chief ordered them to stay put.

By now, the Franklin is a raging inferno. The carrier was beginning to tip to starboard. (*to the right*) "Badly...very badly...a 14 degree list" Just a little more it would go over, and down! "I heard a guy hollering. He was scared. Somebody shut him up, because he was getting panicky."

The Franklin, tipped 14 degrees, a couple more and she would have gone down. This photo was taken from the USS Santa Fe, (CL-60) which came along side, and put her bow against the carrier to keep it from going over.
Photo: US Navy

They let another man in...Marine Private Novak, who had gone out to find a escape route for them. "He was an awful looking mess. He was smoke and blood, from one end to the other." Novak told them they could get out, but they had to go forward."

By now, the passageways were totally filled with black, acrid smoke. Each man wet a cloth to put over their face. The Marine told them, "You're going to have to go on your knees because there's so much junk in the way. Hang onto the belt of the guy ahead of you, and don't let go."

"I don't know how far we got but it was blistering hot." It was slow going," Scotty says, "I can remember that you couldn't see an inch ahead of ya."

It got to him.

"I started to pass out. Leonard Hall, behind me; what he said to me, in the nicest language was, 'Scotty if you quit, I'll kick your ass." Scotty chuckled as he told me, "He grabbed me and got me back on my feet again. I don't think we went another twenty feet, and I could feel cold air."

The carrier was still blowing up, when they got topside. The fire was raging.

The cruiser "Santa Fe" came along side. "That man...that skipper was unbelievable, what he did. He put that cruiser up against the side, where we were tipping over," and kept it from tipping more. The crew of the "Santa Fe" fought the fire. "They were taking the dead and wounded off as fast as they could. Some of um were getting blown off, into the water."

Scotty went to work, fighting the fire. "There must have been four, five hundred men up there...wounded....they were lying on the flight deck." Scotty was one of seven-hundred-and-three crew members who stayed on board the carrier, to fight the fire. He never left.

It was the end of the second day before they got the fire out. Scotty walked around to inspect the damage. He walked by a gun mount near the stern, "There were almost two hundred pairs of shoes there. It was either jump or get blown off the ship. They jumped."

'Big Ben' had drifted to within fifty miles of the Japanese mainland. The carrier was dead in the water...listing to starboard...no radio communications...still in trouble. The USS Pittsburgh got a line her, and slowly towed the carrier away.

Scotty and the engineers got to work, and got some of the boilers fired up. "By the third day we were making 12 knots...we eventually got it up to 22 knots." They got out of there, but for 'Big Ben,' the war was over.

309

They made it back to Pearl Harbor. Enough repairs were done there for the Carrier to make the trip to the Brooklyn Navy yard. There, "They stripped it clear down to the 3rd deck, and rebuilt it."

New York Harbor, April 1945
Church services were held on the damaged hanger deck of the Franklin.
Photo: US Navy

She was anchored in New York Harbor for a few months. The Navy refused a request from the City of New York to make the Franklin into a Jail.

Instead, she was taken to Bayonne, New Jersey and "moth-balled." Scotty was one of the last twenty-six people on board.

There was bitterness in his voice when he told me, "They sold it for scrap" in 1966; sold it for junk."

714 people died on the USS Franklin, that terrible March in 1945. Another 265 were wounded. There were hundreds of "Purple Heart" medals awarded, many more medals of heroism, and two men received the "Medal of Honor."

"U.S.S. FRANKLIN, COMING HOME"
Ernest Scott designed this card for the USS Franklin reunion in Bar Harbor in 2001.
In his message, he talks about the scrapping of the ship, he fought so hard to save, "Much more than steel was obliterated. For us the Franklin was home and hearth. It was life and living. It was church and graveyard. No cutter's torch can sever the ties that we will always have for her, so long as one of us lives."

Like so many others, Ernest Scott came home, and got on with his life.

Since July 21st 1945, Vivian has been part of that life. They celebrated their 61st wedding anniversary in 2006.

Earnest and Vivian Scott. July 21, 1945
Their wedding picture.
Photo: Courtesy the Scotts

Scotty worked at a generating plant, about fifteen miles up the St Croix River, for forty years.

Along the way Ernest wrote the story of his life, "Missed the Saturday Night Dance." about the Woodland he knew, before the war; "We raised hell at the Boom Camp and the Poppul mill. We would listen to Jack Benny, Tom Mix, Jack Armstrong, Amos 'n Andy and Hit Parade," on the radio. Charlie Blaney had the best stealing apples in the world."

He wrote of the heroic battles for life, aboard the Franklin, those terrible days in March, 1945. He told about breakfast, "borrowed from a destroyer," three days after the attack…and about burial detail, "Our dead were everywhere. Some had died quickly and others mercifully. Others died a horribly slow death."

He wrote of Chaplain O'Callahan who received the Medal of Honor, and of Marine Private Novak, who received the Navy Cross. "Those of us,

311

Nolan was a gunner on a half-track. He was with nine others on patrol when a German machine gunner opened up on them. He directed the other men around and away from the fire. He carried one man out on a stretcher, and returned after dark to help another get out. All nine members of the patrol survived. The army awarded Nolan Gibbs the "Bronze Star" for his courageous action that day.

For most veterans, memories of the war are still very much with them. Nolan says a day in 1945 is imbedded in his memory clearest of all. The day they liberated the German concentration camp, "Buchenwald."

Buchenwald 1945

American GI's were overwhelmed at the things they saw at Buchenwald.
The number of
prisoners held at Buchenwald had
exceeded eighty
thousand by April 1945.

Photo: U.S. National Archives

The war was nearly over and the Germans had left by the time the 6th Armored arrived. Nolan says, "We went in and all these bedraggled soldiers with awful ragged uniforms came meeting us..........they were crying."

Nolan returned to his farming duties after the war. Poultry farming was big then. He became the state "Flocks" agent. He got an electrician's license.....training in plumbing and furnace repair. "I did lots of things." He says. "I lived a full life."

Summer 1945.

Nolan Gibbs was part
of the Army of
Occupation in
Germany, after the war
in Europe ended.
Photo: Courtesy,
Nolan Gibbs

NORMAN R. ROSSIGNOL

Bangor, Maine

U.S. Army.........January 1944 – February 1964

S/ Sgt, Infantry

"The Germans... wiped half my squad out."

Norm Rossignol quit high school. He got drafted. A freezing foxhole in the Ardennes Forest was pretty much the next stop for him.

As a kid, Norm used to spend time at a farm up the Bradley Road. "I used to go up there and help milk cows every morning and night." A little extra money came in handy. Things were pretty poor around Old Town those days. Things were pretty poor just about everywhere in 1944.

January 1944, Norm Rossignol was off to Army basic training. "I didn't have any basic training....had two weeks of it." The Army needed him across the ocean.

The Russians had beaten the Germans back at Leningrad. US forces had landed at Anzio, but were stalled at the Gustav line in the Southern Apennine Mountains, in Italy. The Generals were already thinking about Normandy. Depleted infantry forces needed replacements as fast as they could get across the ocean. Norm went across, on the Queen Mary....landed in Scotland.

Norm Rossignol
Europe 1944
Photo: Courtesy: Norm
Rossignol

His 94th Infantry Division landed on Utah Beach on September 8th, 94 days after D-Day. They had been held over in England since his arrival. The Division moved into Brittany, to contain sixty-thousand German troops, surrounded in the Channel ports of Lorient and St Nazaire. Norm says things got hot quickly.

He's had several physicals and no after affects from the radiation. Between July 16, 1945 and September 23, 1992, the US conducted 1,054 nuclear tests, and two nuclear attacks.

Norm Rossignol spent twenty years and a month in the Army. "I think it was the best thing I did in my life," he told me… a life that has turned out pretty good. After the Army he worked as an electrician at the University of Maine; retiring in 1989.

Today, "I snowmobile, ATV, hunt and fish." He talks with students at the Cole Museum. At eighty-one, he's still going strong. "I really enjoy life."

Norman Rossignol
Bangor, Maine, September 2006
Photo: Courtesy Norm Rossignol

KENNETH FERLAND

Bangor, Maine

U.S. Army-Air Corps.................August 1943-March 1946

Sergeant, Gunner

"I'm so thankful for God's help in getting me home safe and sound."

To be lost above the clouds, in an airplane, is about as helpless and hopeless as things get. You know generally where you are, but you can't see the ground. You know there's a landing strip down there, somewhere, but you don't dare go down to find it, because you don't know exactly where it is, and because you don't know where all the hills and tall buildings are either.

That's why one of Ken Ferland's memories from WW II is so interesting and a little bit frightening.

Ken was a gunner on a B-24 bomber during the war, assigned to the 8th Air Force, 453rd Bomber Group stationed at Buckingham, England. A little more about how he got there in a couple of paragraphs, but first, his memories of a day in April 1945.

"We took off with a full bomb load and full tanks of Gas. There were so many bomb groups all over the area, and when we were climbing thru the clouds, you could feel the turbulence from other planes." They couldn't see the other planes, but they felt them. Ken says the brass thought, "We would be able to break out of the soup (clouds) and form up at 14 thousand feet." They were still "souped in" at 14 thousand and continued their climb. It was at that point they lost most of the electronics on the plane, including all the navigational aids. They finally found sunshine at 20 thousand feet, but had no idea where they were. There was nothing but a blanket of clouds as far as they could see, in every direction.

The crew of Ken's B-24 had the added concern of enemy fighters. "All at once we spotted three fighters coming at us. The U.S. P-47 and the

319

WORLD WAR II

1942: Movie star Rita Hayworth sacrificed her bumpers.
The metal was used in the war effort.
Hayworth was also active, selling war bonds.
Photo: National Archives

EARLE L. AUCOIN

Orrington, Maine

U.S. NAVY..........December 7, 1942 – January 6, 1946

Yeoman 1st Class

"We got ninety-two depth charges one time. We were down there for hours."

Earle Aucoin was a submariner during World War II. He was one of those guys who "volunteered" to get into a metal tube, just over three hundred feet long, with a circumference of 27 feet at it's widest point. He would be with seventy or eighty other men, and spend his days under the surface of the ocean; many times the boat would be four or five hundred feet below the surface of the ocean. Earle says, "We were crammed in like a bunch of sardines."

Earle was on the Kittery, Maine constructed "USS Razorback (SS-394)." The keel for the sub was laid down by the Portsmouth Navy Yard on September 9, 1943.

The Razorback was one of 314 submarines that sunk one-thousand-three-hundred and ninety-two enemy vessels during WW II.

The **USS Razorback** in the Pacific, off Hawaii, after WW II.

US Navy photo.

323

World War II – POSTER ART

Rosie the Riveter "We Can Do it."
Poster art by J. Howard Miller
Words, posters and films waged a battle for the
hearts and minds of American citizens during World
War II.
Photo: National Archives

ALBERT W. B. RIPLEY

Brewer, Maine

U.S. Army-Air Force......September 1942 – February 1946

Private First Class, Administrative

"Congratulations, you're in the Air Force."

Al Ripley avoided combat. Credit an old injury, and the need for people to do the things we seldom hear about. Things certainly not as exciting as battle, or as hazardous as ducking bullets in a foxhole, but absolutely necessary for the mission.

Al was in Bangor when he got the call. He was a sheet metal worker at Dow Field...working on aircraft. He had come to Bangor for the job. "All I did was go to work and then I went back and slept. There wasn't too much going on.

Al had attended a school for movie projectionists at the old armory in South Brewer. No real reason, "To learn how to do it." Might come in handy. It did...a little later.

Not a lot going on but he was pretty comfortable with his arrangements and the job at Dow. That was disrupted in mid 1942, and Al's life took a dramatic new direction. "I didn't decide, Uncle Sam decided for me." The infamous draft letter arrived.

The people he worked with at Dow helped decide the direction his military service would take...the people at Dow and that old injury. His supervisor at Dow wrote a letter. "I was working out here at the base and they told me to give them that letter, and I did." Al doesn't even know what the letter said, but when he gave it to the people at the induction center...they looked at it... "Congratulations, you're in the Air Force."

The old injury inserted itself, in Al's, future at basic training in Texas. "The thing is, I've got what they called a ruptured muscle in my left leg, and I forgot to tell um about it when I went in." When they found out, he was assigned to "limited service;" almost the full first year he was in.

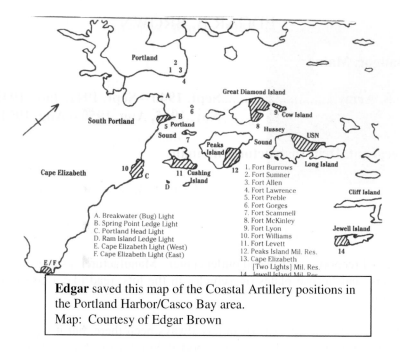

Edgar saved this map of the Coastal Artillery positions in the Portland Harbor/Casco Bay area.
Map: Courtesy of Edgar Brown

Edgar made Sergeant quickly. His promotions accelerated because of his time with the "Coast Artillery." He was made a Cadre Drill Sergeant at Camp Haan in California. Haan was an anti-aircraft artillery replacement center. Edgar trained replacements on the 40 MM anti aircraft gun. The Army sent him to Red Cross school and he learned to be a swimming instructor. He took a three-week course and learned Judo. He also taught that, including hand-to-hand combat.

It wasn't to be all comfortable stateside training for Edgar, however. The Army saw to it that he got training in automatic weapons, and he was made an infantry rifleman, to prepare him for the war. January 1945, he received orders to head for Europe.

Edgar was home on leave in Freeport, preparing for his trip across the ocean, when his family received a telegram from the Army. It said that Edgar's brother Ken had been taken prisoner by the Germans. Ken was with the 106th Division.

Summer 1944: Edgar Brown and his 40 MM gun crew, field training at Camp Irwin in California. Edgar is in the foreground on the right.
Photo: Courtesy Edgar Brown

Edgar remembered getting the news. "On the 19th of February, 1945, I sailed out of New York Harbor on the Queen Mary. Many things went through my mind.....thinking about my brother and wondering what would happen to me. I will never forget the hollow feeling I had in my stomach, sailing by the Statue of Liberty, and watching it go out of sight."

Edgar was a combat "MP" when he reached Europe, assigned to the 92nd replacement depot. He got around a bit, and witnessed the destruction left behind by the guns and the bombs. He also saw places that weren't destroyed. "We went through towns and where they had a white flag, the house was standing and where it wasn't *(a house that had no white flag out the window)* it was blown up."

The war in Europe was nearing the end. There was good news. Ken Brown, Edgar's brother, was liberated from the prison camp by U.S. Forces. He was awarded the P.O.W. Medal and the Bronze Star.

331

WORLD WAR II

Bangor, Maine, June 1944
The sign in the window of the "Bangor Daily Commercial"
announces D-Day, June 6, 1944
Photo: Courtesy Bangor Historical Society

CHARLES HENRY STEVENS

Saginaw, Michigan

U.S. Army.......December 1941 – December 1945

1ˢᵗ Lieutenant, Infantry

"We are thankful that some of us come back."

Yep, this is a book about Maine veterans, and Hank Stevens is not really a Mainer; but if effort and action have any influence, he comes close enough.

You see, at least two dozen times since 1981, Hank and Mary Lou Stevens have climbed in their vehicle and made the two thousand mile round trip from Saginaw, Michigan to attend veteran's activities here in Maine. Until 2006, when Hank couldn't drive the distance anymore, they made every single one of the annual Memorial Day observances at the Cole Land Transportation Museum, and they drove to Bangor for several other special WW II observances too.

Because of that and his attachment to Galen Cole who is very much a Mainer and so important to veterans, Hank's a part of our book. Hank was Galen's lieutenant on a fateful day near the village of Albersloh.

His memory is fading a bit these days but he says the draft got him. Ironically, he was sworn into the U.S Army December 8, 1941, the day after the Japanese attacked Pearl Harbor.

Hank spent his early military years as a trainer. "I was a kind of a gun nut when I was a kid." His grandfather, who liked guns, influenced him. His love of guns as a youngster, determined the early course of his military career. Sometimes it's funny how things happen.

"When they got me in there, they found out that I had been around a gun before."

Hank Stevens 1944
A new 2ⁿᵈ Lieutenant.
Photo: Hank Stevens

The army put him on the range, training others how to shoot. He says he was stuck in the training center for three years and thought he was never going to see the war.

That changed in 1944. By that time Hank had made his way up through the ranks and was a 2nd Lieutenant. He was just the kind of guy who was needed in Europe. Hank was in a group of replacements sent to refill the ranks of the 5th Armored Division: First Platoon, Company B, 46th Armored Infantry Battalion.

It was almost Easter in 1945; Hank's Battalion was chasing the Germans south of Munster. His platoon and a tank platoon were ordered to set up a roadblock. Hank's commander was worried that the Germans would flank them, and come at them from the rear. They were on a road parallel to the road the main convoy was taking, along the Dortmund-EMS Canal, around Munster through Albersloh. They didn't know a German gunner has set up his 88 MM ahead of them. Hank says, "The round went over my head probably about a foot and it came down on the eighth vehicle in the column.... was maybe at that time, three hundred yards behind me." The armor piercing shell solidly grazed the helmet of a medic riding in one half-track....solidly with a capital "Solidly." Hank says, "It made a crease in the top of his steel helmet that you could lay your arm in."

The shell smashed through the passenger side of the steel windshield of the next half-track in line....killing the men sitting on that side, except machine gunner Cliff Lamb. He had bent down to repair his gun. "The machine gun stopped firing." Cliff remembers, "As I reached forward to pull back the operating handle......at that point I just ceased to know anything else." He doesn't know how long he was out. "I woke up, and did not really know what had happened." All the others sitting on the left side of the half-track, including Galen Cole, received shrapnel wounds or broken eardrums.

Stevens spotted the medic with the creased helmet in the ditch. "Of course that knocked him a little bit silly, he didn't know where he was or what was going on." Hank helped him and then went from man to man treating the wounded.....giving shots of morphine.

> **Cliff Lamb** at the Bangor reunion of the 5th Armored Division, September 2000.
> Photo: Cole Museum

They were in a bad spot. Germans gunners had them pinned down. Enemy troops were sneaking between the trees to get behind them. The U.S. tankers bailed them out with their coaxial guns. Hank says, "They knew their job. They started raking that woods back and forth with those guns......they never let up on that trigger until the ammunition can was empty." It gave Hank and surviving members of the platoon time to crawl to better cover.

He says things quieted down then. "The Germans are hiding over there in the trees. We were in our trees. It started to rain, and it was a nasty night......cold rain and we set there with nothing, out there in the wooded area."

When the sun came up the next morning, the Germans were gone. There's an interesting footnote to the story. Hank had taken a "lugar" from a captured German officer. Being a gun man, it was pretty darned important to him. When his squad was ambushed Hank hid the pistol under a stump. After the firing stopped he retrieved it. In 2006 Hank sent the German lugar to Galen Cole. Today the gun is on permanent display in the 5th Armored Division section at the Cole Land Transportation Museum in Bangor.

> **May 1945 Efurt, Germany**
>
> Lt. Charles "Hank" Stevens receives the "Silver Star" from Major General Lunsford Oliver, Cmdr. 5th Armored Division
> Photo: Hank Stevens

In February, General Patton commended the group for work in the reduction of the Ardennes bulge.

The group flew its' one thousandth mission in March, and was in Frankfurt by the middle of April.

They flew their last combat mission, three defensive patrols, on May 9th.

Shady came home in November with enough points to be discharged.

He cooked for twenty years after his military time, and then went to work doing bridge maintenance for the State of Maine, for a few years. Shady spent the last eighteen years of his working life with the Bangor and Aroostook Railroad.

He retired from the railroad, after he lost Evelyn. She died in 1987. They raised eight children.

Evelyn & Shady Blackwell,
mid 80's.
Photo: Courtesy Libby Ireland

DONALD R. SWETT

Howland, Maine

U.S. Army..........................June 29, 1943 – March 28, 1946

Buck Sergeant, Anti Aircraft Artillery

"It was an entirely different world"

"We lost our mother when I was six. We were four children. I was the oldest." Times were tough for the Swett family, of Howland, but Don says they did just fine. "Our grandmother brought us up."

There wasn't a lot of money for traveling, "A trip to Bangor was quite unusual," or money for anything else. "A bottle of pop and a hotdog, you thought you were right in seventh heaven."

Don was only seventeen when he graduated from high school...too young for the military. He got a job at a sawmill, owned by Enos Sawyer...five-dollars-and-68-cents a week...and no coffee breaks. He did get a meal.

Donald Swett
The war years.
Photo: Courtesy Don Swett

As soon as he could, he signed up. The boy from Howland was off to see the world. "It was an entirely different world, especially if you didn't get around much."

Basic training at Camp Hahan, California....Artillery training at Camp Shelby in Mississippi; wow! He even looked up a man in Pasadena his grandmother had brought up in Enfield. "He took us to Grauman's Chinese Theatre." Don had never been south of Bangor.

343

lots of troubles. In fact, by 1944 B-29s would leave the production lines and fly directly to modification depots for extensive rebuilding to incorporate necessary changes.

Ground crew technicians like Crosby then, often had to create miracles to keep their planes in the air. They did their jobs so well, that by the end of the WW II, the B-29s, which were only flown in the Pacific during the war, made a big difference in the outcome. Attacks by the B-29s devastated all large Japanese cities and gravely damaged Japan's war machine.

Harold Crosby, on Guam during WW II.

Certainly, the best known B-29s are the "Enola Gay" which dropped the atomic bomb on Hiroshima and "Bockscar" which dropped the bomb on Nagasaki, three days later.

In a journal he prepared for his children, Crosby says, "We worked twelve hour shifts with no days off." He was stationed on Guam. He goes on to write, "I don't recall any big celebrations following Japan's surrender, but we did go from twelve hour shifts back to working eight hour shifts."

One of the wonderful byproducts of this book, is the opportunity, we get to peek at unique war time experiences in the lives of people like Harold. His wife Iver let me borrow several letters, he sent home to his parents.

Late 1944, Harold had just shipped out of Seattle, heading for the war in the Pacific:

Dear Folks,

"This is another letter in which I can't say very much pertaining to where I am, what I've seen, etc. So you'll have to use your imagination, and do some good guessing. I can't even put the date on this letter."

The envelope is postmarked, December 26, 1944.

In a letter postmarked, January 20, 1945,

"I can't say when, but I've finally arrived safe and sound at my destingation. I think the weather here is ideal, I guess there's ocean breezes all the time."

He was on Guam.

"I was rather surprised to hear of Gram's passing, but I didn't expect to see her again on my return to the states."

August 10, 1945,

"Since we dropped that atomic bomb, it's been the topic of conversation about everywhere one goes, at work, in the mess hall, the showers, etc."

He also writes about a pet monkey one of the guys in the squadron had sent to him from India. Harold like to tell stories about the monkey to students in the Veterans' Interview Program at the Cole Museum. He had been interviewed by more students than anyone else, when he passed away in 2004.

In a letter postmarked October 2, 1945, Harold talks about coming home soon,

"Hope to be home for ice cutting, etc."

He also indicates, hostilities may have not ended.

"The planes left here early this morning for a flight up over Korea, and they were carrying 200 rounds of ammunition per gun. They were told to fire on any plane that fires on them. I've heard say a B-29 was shot down over Korea, after Japan had announced she would surrender."

This story about Harold wouldn't be complete without mention of, Harold Crosby, sports fan. A few days after his death, Bangor Daily News sports columnist, Larry Mahoney wrote, "Crosby was the perfect sports fan."

Mother's Meditation

It matters not how many separating miles
Lie now between my loved sons and me
There is a bond that keeps us close indeed
I am home, you far away, across the sea.

The love we hold, each for the other one
Is precious, deep, enduring, warm, and proud
The faith we share in the Almighty One
Reminds us there is sun behind the cloud.

And though tonight I cannot see your faces
Nor clasp your hands, nor smile into your eyes,
God knows just where to find you anytime,
And hears the prayers that daily for you rise.

I pray God's loving care for my sons
That they be kept high-hearted, clean of soul
With faith and courage that no war can dim
And be returned with minds and bodies whole.

And hearts at home less lonely seem to be
When we commit our loved ones to his care
Knowing that God leans down to bless the two
The one prayed for, and the one who kneels in prayer.

Your Mother
(Hazel Cross)

Russell Bartlett Cross:

On December 7, 1941, Russ Cross was stationed at Schofield Barracks, just outside Hickam Field at Pearl Harbor, Hawaii. He was on observation duty, enjoying a cup of coffee, when he was shocked to see Japanese planes beginning a strafing run. Russ and a buddy actually shot down one of the first Japanese planes.

Not until the next day did Russ learn the horrible devastation from the Japanese surprise attacks on Pearl Harbor, and thus America's entrance into WWII.

Russ was later assigned to the G2 section - intelligence unit - and attended Officer Training School at Fort Bellevoir, Virginia. After school, he returned to Hawaii, and re-joined the 24th Infantry Division. Later joining the 4th Brigade of engineers, Russ trained comrades in

350

amphibious loading and unloading onto beachheads. He never learned to swim. His comrades called him "Captain Chris Cross" and threw him into shark infested waters, just for laughs.

After more training at Ft. Dix, Russell returned to the South Pacific again, and swept Pacific island beaches, assuring safe landings for General Douglas MacArthur. Based in New Guinea for the balance of the war, Russ became a liaison for General MacArthur, traveling between ships in the Pacific.

As a Pratt Institute trained artist, he often sketched MacArthur's activities in the Pacific and was commissioned for an oil painting of him in Hawaii. Many of his drawings were published in the "Army Times."

Russ said, "When they dropped the bombs on Hiroshima and Nagasaki, we opened a can of beer, packed up, and got out of there".

Russell married Jane Migut of New York and worked as an artist for Boston advertising agencies, eventually retiring in Western Massachusetts teaching watercolor painting for many years and showing watercolors at "quite a few" galleries.

William Eben Cross Jr:

In August 1942, William "Bill" Cross enlisted into the U.S. Army Air Force and was assigned to the 35th Photographic Technical Unit, APO 234, in San Francisco, CA.

Upon completing Photo School at Lowry Field, Denver, Colorado, in December 1942, Bill became part of the 6th Photo Squadron at Peterson Field, Colorado Springs, Colorado. Bill went to Bolling Field in Washington, DC, to learn the "Tri-Met" process of mapping.

Arriving in Guam in December, 1944, Bill began printing photos of countless bombing targets in the Pacific, including many in Japan itself, both before and the after a bomb run, to record the damages.

As a member of the 35th Photo Tech Unit, Bill participated in producing more than 1.5 million photo prints, 100 target charts, 1,253 reports, and 1.875 million impressions including General MacArthur's signing of the Japanese peace treaty in Tokyo Harbor aboard the USS Missouri.

With access to transport all around the Pacific Theatre, Bill was able to "arrange" visits with his brothers, Russell in New Guinea and George in Saipan.

After the war, Bill attended Babson Institute on the GI bill and married Helen Prescott of Pennsylvania. Settling in Augusta, Bill worked at Central Maine Power Company, Public Utilities Commission, State of Maine Forestry Department and later became business manager for Baxter State Park.

George Linwood Cross:

George was drafted in January 1943 and left Augusta for Ft. Devens on February 3rd, 1943 along with several other Mainers who remained with George through basic training and the duration of the war.

George arrived in Hawaii on Jan 14, 1944, as part of Battery C, 738th Anti-Aircraft Artillery Gun Battalion. With amphibious and jungle training, George and company left Hawaii on June 2nd with a Task Force for the Marianas. They put into the Marshall Islands while the "Mariana Turkey Shoot" was taking place - U.S. Navy planes destroying the Japanese navy air force.

Saipan, Battery C, 738th Anti-Aircraft Artillery Battalion. (All Maine men.) George Cross is 3rd from the left in the front row in the group picture on the left.

George sailed for Saipan, scheduled to land in the second wave. In route, the ship was "missing in action." It was aground on Penny Island and a sitting duck.

Finally arriving on July 11th, they participated in mop-up operations, from one end of the island to the other. Saipan was finally secured at a cost of 3,100 American lives. Japan began seeing the loss of Saipan as "the beginning of the end".

George was discharged on his birthday, December 18, 1945, and returned to Boston University where he earned his accounting degree and became a CPA. George married Virginia Wise of Gardiner on January 16, 1946. Living in South Portland for many years, George established Cross Professional Associates, CPAs.

Waterville, Maine, October 2, 2001
A reunion of Battery C, 738th Anti-Aircraft Artillery George Cross in on the left in the front row. Bob Glidden, who's story is also in this book is on his right.

This chapter written in part by William F. Cross, the son of George Cross

Photos this chapter, courtesy the Cross Family

Don Colson

SPANISH AMERICAN WAR

Portland, 1898
Volunteers bound for the Spanish American War, march down Congress Street in Portland.
Photo: Maine Historical Society

WILLIAM H. DRISKO

Lincoln, Maine

U.S. Army..........June 1943 – December 1954

Corporal, Infantry/Captain, Battalion Adjutant

"When I first got to Korea, the smell of the place. It smelled bad!"

Bill Drisko's early days in the military were like a lot of other guys.

He graduated from Bangor High School on June 11, 1943.....sworn in on the 17th and was off to Camp Devens on the 30th. "I can recall spending a homesick 4th of July there," he says.

Like many others, Bill was shipped out for special training; in his case, special engineering training at Purdue University. Before he could finish, like a lots of others too, the Army decided it needed riflemen more than it needed engineers and so he was off to the 407th Infantry, 102nd Division at Camp Swift, Texas.

Bill got the experience of a seasick trip across the Atlantic, too.

The Division arrived at Cherbourg, France on September 23, 1944. The 407th moved into Germany from Holland, in late 1944, to relieve troops of the 29th Division. Bill says, "Now it was life in foxholes and cellars, often under fire from enemy 88's and mortars. One mortar round landed so close to my foxhole that shrapnel damaged the rear sight on my M-1 *(rifle)*." The 407th cleared Welz and took Flossdorf in early December 1944.

Drisko volunteered to join a regimental battle patrol. The group was led by Lt. Roy (Buck) Rogers, so it was only natural they would be called "Rogers Raiders:" not to be confused with the famous British unit during the French and Indian War, that gave Army Special Force their name.

Buck Rogers Rangers gave a pretty good accounting of themselves too, making several patrols across the Roer River near Linnich. Bill says they always brought back prisoners.

The 102nd Division crossed the Rhine River at Wesel in early April and moved forward quickly, mopping up resistance behind the 5th Armored Division. On April 14th, the division reached the Elbe River and relieved the 5th Armored. The Division established defensive positions along the river, about fifty miles from Berlin, until hostilities ended on May 7th.

Drisko got out and returned to school again after the war.........forestry at the University of Maine.

Bill took ROTC while he was at Maine, and received a regular army commission as a second lieutenant in the infantry.

That got him back on active duty; to Alaska and eventually to Korea. He was Battalion Adjutant, stationed near the "Demilitarized Zone." What does he remember most about Korea? "When I first got to Korea, the smell of the place. It smelled bad!"

It was at about that time his wife Kay convinced Bill; 'That if the army was going to spell 'career' as Korea, I should resign.' He did, and was discharged on December 19, 1954.

Bill was awarded the "Bronze Star Medal with "V" Device" *(Oak Leaf Cluster)* among several decorations he received while in the military.

He was a forester and then Manager of Logging Operations for Eastern Corporation when that company went out of business. He moved to Great Northern Paper and lived through the downsizing of that company, from Assistant Operations Superintendent, to wood buyer to scaler, so in October of 1989, Bill retired.

In 1998 Bill and Kay moved from Smyrna Mills to Lincoln, to be closer to their family.

Brewer, November 11, 2006
William Drisko preparing to march in the Veteran's Day Parade.
Photo: Courtesy of William Drisko.

GALEN L. COLE

Bangor, Maine

U.S. Army……..July 18, 1944 – February 4, 1946

Buck Sergeant, Infantry

"my community and my fellow man better than I found them."

The sun slipped behind a small cloud as church bells began to echo across the Maine hills.

The sky cleared just as the parade of veterans stepped off down Main Street in Bangor. The applause and cheers of their fellow citizens momentarily drowned out the sound of the bells.

The day was September 2nd, 2005…the 60th anniversary of the end of the war that saved the world, World War II.

At the front of the parade… familiar red sweater… blue "WW II Veteran" baseball cap… walking stick, Galen Cole. I was with him the day he decided the occasion shouldn't pass without a proper observance: he organized the parade, arranged for free lunches for the veterans, and planned the memorial program that followed.

Veterans Remembrance Bridge, Bangor-Brewer, September 2, 1995. Maine Maritime Academy cadets, in the parade on the 50th anniversary of the end of WW II.
Photo: Cole Land Transportation Museum

Galen was at the front of the parade, the day the 'Veteran's Memorial Bridge' between Bangor and Brewer was dedicated and opened. He rode in a jeep that day, with Paul Thibodeau, 92 years old of Bangor, and Alex Civinino, 94 of Millinocket; two veterans of World War I. Largest parade the area had ever seen, some said... until the parade on the 50th anniversary of the end of WW II. Some argued that was larger: yep, Galen organized both of those too.

Even his family has trouble remembering how long Galen has been imagining things... organizing things... making things happen. He was pretty young when he dreamed of building a transportation museum. He was fascinated by vehicles. That dream, lots of hard work and saving, resulted in the Cole Land Transportation Museum in Bangor today.

It may have been the pledge he made near the end of WW II that drives him.

Galen got into the war late; July 18, 1944; a couple of weeks after he graduated from Bangor High School. Like it was for others, basic training at Camp Blanding in Florida was hot and dusty. He found time between basic and the war in Europe to marry his childhood sweetheart, Sue Welch; September 17, 1944.

February 16, 1945 the "Louis Pasteur," an old French liner, pulled away from the pier in New York City; destination Europe and WW II. On board, Galen Cole, a stranger among five thousand. Although the end of hostilities appeared near, the war was still raging ahead of him.

Yalta, February 1945
Winston Churchill, Franklin D Roosevelt and Joseph Stalin.
It was Roosevelt's last major conference. He died of a massive cerebral Hemorrhage, on April 12, 1945.
Photo: National Archives

The big three, Roosevelt of the United States, Churchill of Great Britain, and Stalin of the Soviet Union had just concluded their second conference at Yalta. They talked about how Europe would be divided after the war. They discussed eventual terms of a German surrender. The Germans may have seen the end, but they weren't giving up yet.

The Allies had bulged in the Ardennes *(Battle of the Bulge)* but they didn't break. Casualties were high; US accounts list 19,276 American dead. Replacements were needed everywhere, but the tide had turned. The push was on. Allied forces were nearing the Rhine.

After he had bounced from replacement depot to "repple depple," Galen was assigned to General George Patton's 3rd Army, 5th Armored Division. He had moved so much, his mail from home never caught up. "No mail, no mail, no mail." Seventy-two days he heard that. "Of all the things that happened to me, other than losing my five squad members, no mail during daily mail calls, has had an affect on me for a lifetime."

It was almost Easter. Galen was part of Lt. Henry "Hank" Steven's Platoon, exploring a new route into Germany south of Munster. The convoy paused outside Albersloh. "Hank Stevens was concerned. We waited south of the town for more than an hour. Everyone was uneasy." They had good cause.

The command came, 'move out.' Germans ran for their homes as the tanks and half-tracks came through Albersloh. "We were the first Americans they had seen," Galen says.

The convoy came under fire as they left Albersloh. An armor piercing shell exploded through the passenger side of the half-track. Five of Galen's squad members were killed instantly. "They didn't know what struck them."

Galen and the others, on the driver's side of the half-track, who were still alive, had wounds from shrapnel; some had broken eardrums. "If it had been a high explosive shell it would have killed us all." The survivors crawled, under withering fire, for cover in the ditch.

Galen had shrapnel wounds in his back...wounded but not as bad as some of the others. He says a lot of thoughts went through his head, as he cared for others in that ditch. "I recall praying to my God that if I was fortunate enough to get home from the war, I would do my best to leave my community and my fellow man better than I had found them."

All the wounded were taken to an aid station set up at an elderly German woman's nearby farm... about a mile south of the village. Mrs. Hagemann helped medics clean and bandage the wounds of the many survivors of that fighting. Her humanitarian work, that day, made a lasting impression on Galen. After the war he returned to thank her. One of her granddaughters has since visited the Coles in Maine. It was just before Christmas 2006 when I interviewed Galen for this book. He called the Hagemann family in Germany while I was there. He asked the granddaughter to say a prayer over Mrs. Hagemann's grave.

Galen headed back to his platoon, after a few weeks in an Army hospital. The 5th was forty miles from Berlin. He had been in Europe for almost three month, wounded, hospitalized and still hadn't received mail.

Erfurt, Germany 1945. Galen Cole sitting on a half-track at the railroad station. The war was finally over. Photo: Cole Museum

The division had dug in near Stendel, on the Elbe River. Galen could hear the shelling as he caught up with the fifth. The war would have to wait. The mail carrier was his first priority.

Finally!

Galen says he didn't even take time to sort the nearly one hundred letters. He just began reading. Finally, he had word from his family.

Tec 4, Galen Cole was discharged from Military Service on February 4, 1946. His discharge says he served in England, France, Belgium, Holland, Luxembourg and Germany. He was awarded the Combat Infantry Badge and "The Military Order of the Purple Heart." *(In 2002, the "Military Order of the Purple Heart" awarded its' top Americanism award to Galen.)*

Galen met Sue in Boston. They hadn't seen each other for over a year. Boston hotels were full. A chance encounter with Massachusetts State Senator Robert Lee changed that for them. He arranged for a room at the Parker House. .

Galen went back to Coles Express when he got home; the company his father and mother, Allie and Amy Cole had created almost thirty years earlier with a horse and buggy and their life savings. Nine years after the

the war, after his father's death, Galen's brothers elected him President of the company. Galen was twenty-nine years old. He built Coles Express into one of the most respected and successful trucking companies in the Northeast.

Galen returned to Europe several times to visit the graves of his squad members who are buried in the Margraten American Cemetary in Holland. The graves were adopted and cared for by Holland Citizen Henk Dideriks; one of thousands of that country's citizens who care for the 8,301 graves.

May 1992, Galen Cole at Margraten U.S. Military Cemetery in Luxembourg

Margraten Cemetary, Holland
The gravesite of P.F.C William Golliday at Margraten Cemetary in Holland. Cole and Golliday had switched seats on the half-track as the convoy prepared to move out toward Albersloh.

Through a new friend, Const Goergen, U.S. Veterans Friends, Luxembourg was developed. They now decorate the 5,076 graves of American service personnel in the Hamm U.S. Military Cemetery in Luxembourg twice a year. They selected Galen Cole to be their "Honorary President." "I wouldn't pass that up for the Governorship of Maine," Galen told me.

Luxembourg June 2004
Galen Cole and Const Goergen, President "U.S. Veterans Friends-Luxembourg"
Photos this page : Courtesy Cole Museum

361

Galen and Sue have spent their life making their community and their fellow man better than they found them. Galen's boyhood dream of a Museum is a reality today. The several hundred vehicles and displays are believed to be the largest-collection of one state's *(Maine)* land transportation history anywhere in the country.

Cole Land Transportation Museum, Bangor
On September 17, 2006 Galen and Sue Cole celebrated their
sixty-second wedding anniversary.
(The car is a 1931 REO Royale Coupe, on display at the museum.
It's one of only twelve still in existence.)
Photo: Courtesy the Coles

It's no surprise the museum also includes an exhibit dedicated to the 5th Armored Division, complete with a half-track, and over a hundred other artifacts.

The State of Maine World War II monument was constructed and dedicated on museum grounds, along with a Vietnam Monument and Memorial complete with a huey helicopter.

The "Veteran Interview Program" for Maine students, mentioned by a number of the veterans in this book, takes place at the museum.

The Military Order of the Purple Heart.
The "Purple Heart was originally established by General George Washington of the Continental Army. It was awarded during the Revolutionary War, and then revived in World War I.
Photo: US Army

The State of Maine Military Order of the Purple Heart Memorial is also located on museum grounds.

Each year the Freedom Foundation at Valley Forge presents awards to a select few in America, for their work promoting freedom.

The award is based on a "Bill of Responsibilities:"

"Freedom and responsibility are mutual and inseparable; we can ensure enjoyment of the one only by exercising the other. Freedom for all of us depends on responsibility by each of us. To secure and expand our liberties, therefore, we accept these responsibilities as individual members of a free society."

On Veterans Day 1992, Maine Chief Justice, Retired, Vincent McKusick presented the award to Galen Cole.

One of the most memorable times happened in 2005.

Galen realized many of Maine's vets might never be able to go to Washington, D.C. to see the new National WW II Memorial. David Fink, President of Pan Am Airlines provided a plane... Galen arranged the rest, and on September 23rd seventy-nine veterans were able to make the trip; forty-one of them veterans of World War II. Galen also invited more than fifty Bangor troop greeters, very much patriots, to go along.

I'll never forget the tears, as old war hardened veterans were overcome by their emotion.

Washington, D.C. September 23, 2005
Maine veterans at the WW II Memorial. Governor John Baldacci
is just left of center. Galen Cole is to his right.
Photo: Cole Museum

That night, as their plane neared Bangor and home, someone in the back started singing "God Bless America." The entire plane joined in. It was a special day!

THANKS AND ACKNOWLEDGMENTS

First of all, thanks to all the veterans. Thanks for providing your stories and pictures. Thanks for what you did.

Almost to a person, when I asked about your experiences, the answer minimized your actions. "I didn't do anything." "I did what I had to do." In fact, you did a lot. You protected our precious freedom, and our way of life.

You were on the front lines, or standing alert at the end of some isolated runway, or patrolling the oceans. Thousands of others made it possible for you to be there. Our potential enemies knew it. Because of you; our children and grandchildren are free to live their lives, free to pursue their dreams. You did a lot!

Thanks to A Mark Woodward of the Bangor Daily News, and Alan Baker of The Ellsworth American, for the use of your pictures; and to Roxanne Moore Saucier for helping get the word out...three of the best "News" people, I ever met.

And for photos, information, and other assistance, thanks to:

Stars and Stripes
St Petersburg Times
Naval Institute Press
The Downeast Coastal Press/Chessie Johnson
"Paper Talks" Magazine
Bangor "Metro" magazine
Bangor Convention and Visitors Bureau
Bangor International Airport/Dawn Little
The Town of Greenville
The Town of Lincoln
Maine Secretary of State
Maine Historical Society
Bangor Historical Society
University of Minnesota
Marist College
Harry S. Truman Presidential Library
Franklin D. Roosevelt Presidential Library
Medal of Honor Society
86th Blackhawk Division

THANKS AND ACKNOWLEDGMENTS, Cont.

101st Air Refueling Wing, ME ANG, Major Deborah Kelley
Submarine Sailor
Outpost Harry Survivor's Association
VFW Post # 10216, Song Si, So Korea
James Aldrich

Special thanks to Senator Susan Collins and Governor John Baldacci for writing "Forewords" for this book. It's a bit unusual to have two "Forewords" but both are great supporters of our veterans, and this book would not have been complete without their words.

Thanks to, Galen Cole, for the inspiration and support for this project. Thanks for asking me to do it.

Thanks to Gary Cole for proof reading and catching most of my mistakes.

Thanks to Lowell Kjenstad, Pat Trice, and Ben Ayott of the Cole Museum for digging out all the additional information, and pictures, and all the other assistance along the way.

Thanks to all the folks at J.S. McCarthy Printers who were so helpful, particularly Shawn Anderson, who fixed pictures, my mistakes, and bailed me out of a bunch of disagreements with my computer, Ralph Lizotte for making the cover better than I could have imagined, and Joe Bedard for patiently pulling everything together.

And thanks to my wife Brenda for allowing the kitchen renovations to wait, so I could finish this book, and for allowing me time to sit at my computer all day, so many days.